Redefining Humanism

SELECTED ESSAYS OF D.P. MUKERJI

Redefining Humanism

SELECTED ESSAYS OF D.P. MUKERJI

Edited by
SROBONA MUNSHI

 Tulika Books

in association with the
University of Calcutta

Published by **Tulika Books**
35 A/1 (third floor), Shahpur Jat, New Delhi 110 049, India

First published in India 2009

Reprint 2012

ISBN: 978-93-82381-07-5

Typeset in Sabon at Tulika Print Communication Services,
New Delhi; and printed at Chaman Offset, Delhi 110 002

Contents

Foreword

Professor D.P. Mukerji (1894–1961)—DP Sahab or DP, as he was generally known with respect and affection—was already in the sunset years of his long and distinguished teaching career at the University of Lucknow when I became his student there in the early 1950s. He was a charismatic teacher attracting students across faculties. It was his lectures and informal conversations that led us to his English books (five monographs and three collections of essays) and to his articles in magazines, such as the *Swarajya* (Madras), and newspapers, notably the *National Herald* (Lucknow). Its renowned editor, Mr Chalapathi Rao, who was DP's friend and admirer (they met almost every evening at the Coffee House), hailed him as one of the 'glories' of Lucknow University.

The quality that most distinguished DP from other teachers, it seemed to many of us, was the conviction with which he put across to us the idea that the life of the intellectual was a challenge and a life truly worth living. It meant engagement with the adventure of ideas, but it was not a retreat into the ivory tower or the cloister. Unlike the bureaucracy (the IAS had emerged as an attractive career option), it promised a life of freedom and creativity, and unlike politics, it offered the life of responsibility and social virtue. In his vision of India's future, intellectuals, particularly those in the universities (research institutes had not yet made their appearance), were going to be significant role players.

Austere of countenance and rather frail in body (years later when I saw Houdon's Voltaire, the intensity of his expression put me in mind of DP), he was a passionate and critical thinker who encouraged us to take nothing for granted. The bane of intellectual creativity of India's public affairs, he used to tell us, had been Gandhiji's 'inner voice' and the Left's 'Party Line'! For himself, he once told me, there were few joys greater than to see the 'blossoming' of young minds.

Although the spoken rather than the written word was by common consent his forte, he was no mean writer in English. (He had not, however, exercised good judgement, it seemed to me, in the choice of the pieces that he had included in the three volume of articles). In Bengali, I understand, he was a prose writer of distinction, essayist, novelist and short story writer. Those of us who do not read Bengali are now deeply beholden to Professor Srobona Munshi and her colleagues (all teachers of English) at the University of Calcutta, Presidency College and Lady Brabourne College (both at Kolkata), for providing us with excellent English translations of eight essays selected from DP's collection *Baktabya* (1957).

I will not discuss the essays here as Srobona Munshi has done this with care and felicity of expression in her editorial introduction. I will only highlight a few general themes of DP's Bengali writings included in the present volume. I had also known his intellectual concerns from his English writings and from personal contact with him, which lasted just over a decade. His last composition in English (written late in 1960 at my request) was a brief tribute to his friend D.N. Majumdar. Reading the essays comprising this book has revived, if at all such revival was needed, my remembrance of DP as an intellectual, scholar and author.

The first thing I would like to highlight is the broad range of DP's interests, which was nourished by both his vast scholarship and his sharp critical acumen. Daring us to broaden our minds, he used to rhetorically ask how we believed we could be good sociologists, that is students of social institutions, if we did not know their history, and how we thought we could be good students of history if we did not have a philosophy of history. This goading was ceaseless: when had we last been to a music concert; had we seen 'The Death of a Salesman': what did we think of it; what books had we been reading, but surely we knew that life was not about books but experience. And authentic experience required a holistic perspective. (Incidentally, Mr Ram Advani, Lucknow's famous bookseller, has written in a published article that it was DP who suggested to him to extend credit facilities to me when I was still a student.)

Specialization was for DP an abomination. He considered the unity of knowledge and the integrated life inseparable; in fact, he used to say that he was willing to be 'dragged to the stake' if his view was considered apostatical in the era of rigid disciplinary boundaries. He did not totally deny the pedagogic usefulness of disciplinary divisions, but emphasized the importance of gathering together the harvests—a task that he wanted sociologists to make their own. He used to call sociology (somewhat inelegantly, I am afraid!)

the 'n+1th science'. One way to do this was to focus on thematic rubrics that inevitably spilled out of disciplinary boxes.

One such thematic focus was culture. His magnum opus in English was *Modern Indian Culture* (1942–48). He considered the anthropological concept of culture, and the empiricism and relativism that went with it, useful, but (to use one of his favourite phrases) only up to a point. It acted, he wrote in one of his essays, as 'a great shock absorber' and promoted tolerance (*Diversities*, 1958, p. 261). Anthropology would, however, amount to nothing more than an exercise in description unless it concerned itself with the remaking of culture (ibid., p. 265), and this essentially entailed a concern with values or, to put it in words of DP's choice, 'the philosophical attitude'. Culture ultimately was, he believed, about matters of style and taste, about discrimination and selection. We were spoken to about Ruth Benedict's formal (aesthetic) theory of cultural integration and persistence (*Patterns of Culture*), and about Malinowski's thesis of the mutual implication of freedom and civilization (*Freedom and Civilization*). Stepping outside anthropology, we were invited to consider Matthew Arnold's emphasis (in *Culture and Anarchy*) on the place of theoretical speculation and ideals of moral conduct ('sweetness and light') in *literate* (as against pre-literate) cultures.

DP did not shy away from the notion of levels of culture, for him it was a question of values, and like Nietzsche (who is cited in one of the essays in this book), he had a horror of nihilism. In DP's judgement, vulgarity was unquestionably a more serious threat to the decent life, to culture, than obscenity. It was the duty of the intellectuals to defend culture in every domain—at home and work; in the concert hall, the gallery and the theatre; in literature and in the sciences. Self-consciousness was the heart of the matter; 'the responsibility to increase awareness . . . rests squarely with the intellectuals, and with no one else' (p. 62 below).

In short, culture was concerned with perfection, with self-education. To clarify by comparison, the idea was, I think, the same as what the Germans of yesteryears called *Bildung* (and DP knew his Goethe); the Greeks of course knew it as *paideia*. In India in the twentieth century, DP hailed Tagore as the best exemplar of the ideal (*Tagore: A Study*, 1943/1972). Rooted firmly in tradition, Tagore was therefore strong enough to confront the West and to adopt from it selectively, indeed creatively. It was thus that his achievements as a man of culture were superior to those of both Bankim and Gandhi. He set high standards and escaped the crippling clutches of the artificially created (under colonialism), mimetic Indian middle class. Its culture was spurious, lacking in authenticity; Tagore's creativity was wholly genuine.

The relationship of the intellectual elite and the masses was, DP argued, crucial to the development of modern Indian culture. It had to be hierarchical; the elite had to instruct. (One of the books he asked us to read and ponder was José Ortega y Gasset's *The Revolt of the Masses*, which, although about Europe, told a cautionary tale of general applicability of how masses let loose can produce widespread demoralization in society.)

In 'Intellectuals and Society', written in 1947–48, DP observed: 'Some sort of independence has at last been achieved—so, what should be our [intellectuals'] duty now? The answer to this question has to be found quickly and so simply and beguilingly communicated to the masses that they believe it to be in their own self-interest and accept it of their own free will' (p. 56). The intellectuals have to be the leaders. They have to refine the thinking of the masses, which (as Mao Tse-tung told André Malraux) tends to be sound though confused, and return its essence to them clearly articulated.

The true leaders, in DP's scheme of life, never acted for themselves, but on behalf of the group and eventually society. The leader was not an individual (*vyakti*)—individualism was the scourge of Western society—but a Person, *purusha*, and his task was *purushakara*. This idea elaborated into an ideology was called *Purushavad* by him, 'Personalism' in Srobona Munshi's translation. I would rather call it the ideology of Human Agency: 'Men make their own history', according to Marx, 'but they do not make it just as they please'. Even so, within the limits set by 'circumstances . . . transmitted from the past' (the historical situation), *they make it*. History moves in its own steam towards the next higher stage, but, DP maintained, it can be given a push and steered in a particular direction: 'every intellectual and intelligent man has the duty of constructing the right attitude to history' (p. 66 below). To say so meant, in Srobona Munshi's apt words, having 'faith in humanity and faith in history'. And since 'man is at the centre of Marxism', to hold such a view was, DP believed, in consonance with Marxism: 'Marxism is a modern version of the old Humanism' (p. 54).

Marxism was, of course, one of the abiding themes of DP's work and this interest is well reflected in the essays selected for this volume. He refused, however, to be called a Marxist; the most he allowed was the designation of Marxologist. It fitted with his temperament and his role as a teacher. The uncritical textbook Marxists of India infuriated him, but he saw a historical role cut out for them; hence his concern about Left unity, which finds expression in this volume.

Almost reversing his argument about the leadership role of intellectuals, DP believed that the Left leadership would fulfil its role under pressure from below, the peasants and the workers. One would have liked to have the two positions (about the role of leadership) not merely reconciled (DP's dialectical approach had bigger goals) but transformed into a higher synthesis. But then the scope of an essay is limited by its length. Moreover, DP often wrote under the pressure of the prevailing circumstances, and as these changed, this analysis also underwent a change. Many of the essays in this volume will seem dated (is the issue of Left unity dated?) to the readers, but their value lies in their being a commentary on changing times. The unity of the essays is conceptual and methodological. They are an important chapter in the intellectual history of modern India.

One last point before I conclude. DP has had his admirers but also his critics. One of the major grounds of criticism has been that in his conception of Indian culture the Hindu tradition is bestowed hegemonic status. From this perspective, the relationship of the Hindus with the various 'others' is that of patronage. Thus, DP argued that, in independent India, Muslims must be allowed political and social space, with opportunities for participation in culture (see pp. 59–60 below). His ideology of *Purushavad* also could be said to have Brahmanical roots. It is criticism that one would have liked him to answer. Maybe he thought that the cultural tradition with the longest history and the widest spread provided the most viable basis for the making of a significant cultural synthesis, that without it there would only be local experiments. But there had been, as he discussed in *Modern Indian Culture*, serious obstacles in the way of achieving such a synthesis in full measure, notably the lack of congruence of the primary values of the different traditions in the medieval period, and later, the negative impact of colonialism. The superficial character of some post-independence ventures in the field of culture generally left him cold, and at times even distressed. He did not, however, live long enough to make firmer judgements.

In the Preface to *Diversities*, D.P. Mukerji wrote (obviously teasingly) that his Bengali friends had 'ignored' his English books, and his non-Bengali friends 'had not read the Bengali ones'! In the latter conclusion he was of course right. When the present volume becomes available, the non-Bengali readers will have had one of their longstanding wishes fulfilled. I thank Srobona Munshi and her colleagues for their labour of love and compliment them for their love of scholarship. It is indeed a pleasure to commend *Redefining Humanism: Selected Essays of D.P. Mukerji* to the readers, including those who may have read these compositions in the original Bengali.

T.N. MADAN

Preface

This book is the outcome of a project undertaken as part of the UGC sponsored DRS (SAP III) programme of the Department of English, University of Calcutta. The context in which the project took off was the production of source material in English for research in the area of literary and cultural exchange between Bengal and Britain in the last two centuries. My choice of D.P. Mukerji's sociological writings in Bengali as material for translation was the result of several factors. Although the last post that he held was as Professor and Head of the Department of Economics at Aligarh Muslim University, it was as a pioneer in the study of sociology in India that D.P. Mukerji is better known in academic circles. Well versed in Indian history and philosophy, he was also conversant with the rational thought and liberal values of the so-called Western Enlightenment. His mind and work thus became the eclectic meeting ground of the intellectual traditions of India and the West. His books in English are well known to students of sociology. But his Bengali writings on social issues are as yet unknown to his non-Bengali readers. The essays translated in this book, it is believed, will thus provide additional material for interested scholars.

The eight essays translated in this volume are taken from a collection entitled *Baktabya*, roughly translated as 'Statements', published in 1957. They were composed much earlier. The five essays in Part One of the present volume were written between 1947 and 1949 while the three essays in Part Two first appeared in the years 1933 to 1935. The latter three though written earlier are placed after the first five not only because that is how they appear in *Baktabya* but because this seems to be the proper arrangement. The author's emphasis on history and the scientific interpretation of history in the five essays of the first Part seems to culminate, as it were, in his exegesis of the meaning and method of history in the three essays of the second Part. A simple working glossary has been compiled from secondary sources and appended at the end in the interest of the reader for D.P. Mukerji did not provide notes or references in his writings. Only such names mentioned in the essays as are not very widely known have been included in the glossary. Also, we have not been able to trace some of the mentioned authors and, as the names appear in the essays in the Bengali script, we are not even sure if we have spelt them correctly in the English transcription.

I am grateful to all the translators of the essays for their enthusiastic participation in the project, their timely submission of manuscripts and above all for their patience. Professor Sanjukta Dasgupta wishes to acknowledge her debt to Dr Dipannita Datta for her invaluable assistance in translating the essay 'Further Thoughts on Faith in Man'. Professor Jharna Sanyal would like to thank Ms Paromita Sanyal for her help in translating 'For Personalism: Against Individualism'. Ms Debjani Roy Moulik has assisted me in my editorial work as has Ms Chandosi Sanyal and I am very thankful to both of them. Professor Krishna Sen, Coordinator of the first phase of the DRS programme and Professor Tapati Gupta, former Head of the Department of English, have both given me their unstinted cooperation at all times. Professor T.N. Madan, one of the most distinguished scholars to have been taught by D.P. Mukerji, has put me in his debt by graciously writing a Foreword for this book. I am indebted to Professor Alok Ray whose biography of D.P. Mukerji in Bengali has supplied me with many details of his life. I have also benefited from the learned introductions by Professor Saroj Bandyopadhyay, Professor Ujjwal Kumar Majumdar, and the late Ananta Kumar Chakrabarty to the *Collected Works* in Bengali of D.P. Mukerji in three volumes published by Dey's Publishing, Calcutta, 1985–1987. Special mention must be made of the moving tribute written for the last of these volumes by the eminent economist Professor Ashok Mitra who was much influenced by D.P. Mukerji. I would also like to thank Ms Indira Chandrasekhar, Rani Ray and Devalina Mookerjee of Tulika Books for all their help and for doing their part of the job so well. Finally, I wish to express my gratitude to Professor Suranjan Das, Vice-Chancellor of the University of Calcutta, for his interest in our work and for helping it to see the light of day.

Kolkata, 2009   SROBONA MUNSHI

Introduction

Dhurjati Prasad Mukerji, affectionately called DP by his students and admirers, has commanded the respect of all those who have known him either personally or through a study of his writings. He wrote in English as well as in Bengali. Those who have read his writings in English have been, by and large, uninformed about his Bengali writings. The purpose of this book is to overcome this problem by making available in English some of his Bengali essays. These essays were written during the years of the Freedom Movement and Independence. Though some of his immediate concerns have receded into the background, his major engagement in these essays deserves a fresh look. This engagement, as the title of the book suggests, is to redefine humanism. He examines humanism with reference to both European and Indian thought and concludes that in this age of the erosion of faith in God what is needed is faith in man. But this faith in man must go beyond that of thinkers such as Rousseau or Gandhi. DP proposes here an interesting idea, the idea of *purushavada* which can be roughly translated as personalism. DP pursues this idea in relation to history. The importance of history lies in showing us that even a philosophical outlook has to be considered in its historical context. Just as it is necessary to have faith in man, it is necessary to have faith in history. And history reveals to us that man is unable to attain full humanity mainly because of class divisions. DP's engagement with humanism thus has a contemporary relevance. Even a reader who has carefully studied his writings in English will find much that is valuable in these Bengali essays written more than fifty years ago.

DP was born on 5 October 1894 in Srirampur in Bengal's Hooghly district, the original home of his grandmother on the father's side. The male line of the family came from Narayanpur, close to Bhatpara, in what is now the district of North 24 Parganas. DP's father Bhupatinath, a law graduate of the University of Calcutta, practised law at the Alipur–Barasat court and made Barasat his permanent place of residence. Bhupatinath's father, Kalidas Mukhopadhyay, had been the Headmaster of Hooghly Branch School and, later, Assistant Professor at Hooghly College where he earned renown as a teacher of English and History at a time when not many Indians were appointed to teaching posts. Among his students were Syed Amir Ali, Hon'ble Justice Shamsul Huda and Hon'ble Justice Zahid Suhrawardy. DP's mother Elokeshi Devi was the daughter of Hemchandra Chattopadhyay who was a favourite student of Alexander Duff. An M.A. in Philosophy from Calcutta University, Hemchandra taught in Hooghly College before he turned to law, taking up practice at the Hooghly Court where he became exceptionally eminent in the field of Criminal Law.

The eldest son of his parents, DP studied mainly at Barasat Government School and for a short while at Hare School in Calcutta. He passed his Entrance examination in 1909 and stood first in the university in English and Sanskrit. However, his inclination for science made him take up the Intermediate Science course in St. Xavier's College, Calcutta. Missing a year on account of illness, he took the examination in 1912 from Ripon College where he also enrolled for the B.A. degree with Honours in English but with Mathematics and Chemistry as subsidiary subjects. Securing first class marks in English and fairly good marks in Mathematics, he failed in his Chemistry practicals, allegedly for losing time while helping out a fellow student! His association with Ripon College was of great significance for he found there some of the foremost teachers of his time who left a powerful impression on his young mind. About this time DP fell seriously ill. He went to Darjeeling to recuperate and it was there that he met and came to know at close quarters the philosopher Acharya Brajendranath Seal. Meanwhile, DP's father had decided to send him to England to complete his education at the London School of Economics. Accordingly DP set sail for England but fell so sick on the way that he had to come back home from Colombo. A year passed by in sickness and depression but he finally appeared for his BA examination in 1916 from Bangabasi College, Calcutta. After graduation he took up the MA course in History at the University of Calcutta and simultaneously the study of law at the Law College of the same university. Abandoning the law course, he somehow managed to take the MA examination in History in 1918 which he cleared without great distinction. His indifference to studies this time was induced by psychosomatic disorders exacerbated by the death of his second brother a few months before the examination. DP was later to dedicate *Personality and the Social Sciences*, his first published book, to the memory of this brother. He later recalled how much he was helped during this trying time by his lifelong friend Satyendranath Bose whom the world knows as a physicist but whose range of learning and skills seemed phenomenal to those who knew him closely. In July 1919, DP married Chhaya Devi, daughter of Probodh Chandra Bandyopadhyay; their son Kumar, an only child, was born in February 1927. DP earned his second MA degree in 1920 in Economics (then known as Political Economy) and was placed second in the first class. His father had died shortly before the examination.

In this first phase of his life, DP was greatly influenced by several members of his family and by his teachers in Ripon College. His father had been a student of science with a good command of English language and literature. DP's interest in History was inherited from his father and his paternal grandfather. His respect for science was due to the influence not only of his father but also of Professor Satish Chattopadhyay of City College and of Acharya Ramendrasundar Trivedi of Ripon College who contributed the scientific temper and methodology to DP's intellectual equipment. Music was possibly the greatest love of DP's life. His admiration for the serene purity of *dhrupad* was in line with his father's distinct preference for that pristine form of Indian classical music. DP's mother came from a family of music lovers. She herself was a good singer of *tappas* and her father's house was a seat of soirées of classical music. Her nephew and DP's cousin Tripuracharan Chattopadhyay (whom the younger members of the family called Tipuda) had a melodious and sonorous singing voice. An MA in philosophy and a sceptic, Tipuda was the friend, philosopher and guide of DP's youth. As for his teachers, DP was singularly fortunate in being taught by a galaxy of them, the best in Bengal of that era. In his *Reminiscences*, DP writes about the heady mixture of a variety of intellectual fare that he was exposed to. He writes of Ishan Ghosh's teaching of History in school; of Acharya Ramendrasundar, Janakinath, Kshetramohan, of Aghor Chattopadhyay's Chemistry classes in college; of Henry Stephen and Manmohan Ghosh and their English lectures and of the philosopher Brajendranath Seal at the University of Calcutta; of the association with Pramatha Chowdhury, the doyen of Bengali prose writers, with Rabindranath Tagore and Patrick Geddes; of the distant light shed by Acharya Jagadishchandra Bose and Acharya Prafullachandra Roy; and of the hovering presence of Abanindranath and Gaganendranath with their art and of Radhika Goswami, Keramat Khan, Viswanath Rao with theirs. 'All of them, I thought, were telling me not to be satisfied with small things', DP wrote.

After his second MA, DP taught for a year in Bangabasi College. Sir Asutosh Mukherjee, then Vice-Chancellor of the University of Calcutta, had planned to induct DP as a lecturer into his own university and had made his intention known. The plan did not materialize. DP recounted later that when Sir Asutosh told him why he had been denied and the job had gone to another, he felt nothing but admiration for a man whom he had always respected. Anyhow, Calcutta's loss was Lucknow's gain for at this time Professor Radhakumud Mukherjee brought him over to Lucknow University where DP spent the next thirty two years of his life, first as Lecturer, then as Reader, and finally as Professor of Economics and Sociology. It was in Lucknow that DP established himself as one of the foremost intellectuals of his time. His lectures revealed the vast sweep of his knowledge but DP did not stop at mere dissemination of knowledge. He strove to stimulate the minds of his students. His teaching was inspirational, as many generations of his students have testified. Some of DP's fellow teachers at Lucknow were Radhakumud Mukherjee and his brother Radhakamal Mukherjee, Bhujangabhushan Mukherjee, Dhiren Mazumdar, B.N. Dasgupta, Sailen Dasgupta, N.K. Siddhant, Birbal Sahni and Wali Muhammad. Together they shaped Lucknow University into an institution of great eminence and repute in the middle decades of the last century. Among DP's distinguished students and younger associates were Nurul Hassan, P.C. Joshi, T.N. Madan, Ashok Mitra, Khaleq and Shafiq Naqvi, Raghunath Reddy, A.K. Saran, and V.B. Singh. DP never studied for a doctoral degree—his mind was perhaps too restless to undertake the rigours of sustained research—but he was always in touch with the latest research in the social sciences. Whatever he read he would then subject to intense sceptical inquiry. When teaching, DP preferred the interactive mode, for his attempt was to instil in his students the values of intellectual curiosity and inquiry which he believed were the best part of all old traditions and new endeavours. The enrichment was not a one-way process, for DP too developed as he taught. Personality was not just a concept that emerged in the course of his sociological discourses. He engaged his own personality in his reading, writing, teaching, arguing, and listening. And in that personality the inclination for scientific thinking was harmonized with aesthetic appreciation and creativity; rationality and cerebration were tempered by emotional involvement and sympathy. DP strove to be and was a scholar in the humanistic mould.

During his tenure at Lucknow University, DP lent his services twice to the U.P. Government, once in 1938 as Director of Information, and again in 1947 as Member of the U.P. Government Labour Enquiry Committee. In 1949 DP was appointed Professor at the insistence of Acharya Narendra Deb, the then Vice-Chancellor of Lucknow University. The fact that it took twenty-seven years for the professorship to come his way was a matter that he refused to accept as demeaning. 'To be a Lecturer was honour enough for me. I never aspired for anything higher . . . these class distinctions have no value for me', he wrote in his diary towards the end of his life. However, it was from this time till his death that DP enjoyed the most glorious period of his life. His first visit to Europe took place in 1952 when he went to the Soviet Union for three months as a member of a delegation. The next sojourn abroad was in The Hague as Visiting Professor at the newly founded Institute of Social Studies for seven months in 1953–54. During this time he was invited for lectures and seminars at different centres in Europe, including Oxford and Paris. In August 1955, DP participated in the Bandung Conference where he spoke on the role of the co-operative movement in economic planning. Before this, after his return from Europe, DP had retired from Lucknow University and joined Aligarh Muslim University at the request of Dr Zakir Hussain as Professor and Head of the Department of Economics. In his five years at Aligarh, DP tried to build up the department with all the energy and diligence he could command in his frail state of health. In December 1955, DP was diagnosed with cancer of the throat for which he underwent surgery in May of the following year in Canton Spital in Zurich. Retiring from Aligarh Muslim University on 30 September 1959, DP decided to live for the rest of his days in Dehra Dun with summers spent in Calcutta. Rapidly deteriorating health forced him back to Calcutta in November 1961. On 5 December 1961 DP breathed his last. Chhaya Devi, revered as Maaji by DP's students, died on 1 January 1998.

It was as a member of Pramathanath Chowdhury's Sabuj Patra group that DP made his first foray into writing in the mother tongue. Pramatha Chowdhury led his group from the front, writing most of the articles for his monthly *Sabuj Patra* with Rabindranath Tagore as the other principal contributor. Pramathababu was not just a writer himself, he possessed the remarkable faculty of moulding new writers. There would be regular meetings in his house of established writers and budding talents. The topics discussed were diverse but mostly centred on social issues, and the mode of discussion was by means of argument and counter-argument. No sooner would someone make a proposition than there would be someone to refute it. This kind of disputation widened the mental horizons of the participants and sharpened their intellect. The dialectical mode of thinking honed during these discussions found its way into the pieces which the members wrote and contributed to the journal. This was the coming of age in Bengali literature of the genre of the serious essay—highly innovative in the choice of topics and style of presentation. DP's early apprenticeship under Pramatha Chowdhury determined the future course not only of his non-fictional prose but of his novels and stories as well. His first publication was *Dadar Diary* (*Elder Brother's Diary*). It was about his Tipuda, mentioned earlier, and it was published in three parts in *Sabuj Patra* in 1916–17. With his critical and creative talents released, DP started writing for other journals too, notably *Uttara* and *Bichitra*. The journal with which the later DP was intimately associated was *Parichay* edited by the poet Sudhindranath Datta. Like *Sabuj Patra*, *Parichay* attracted the best contemporary talent and, again like its predecessor, nurtured the minds of young intellectuals by setting high standards, which would be achieved through intensive dialogue and discussion in Sudhindranath's parlour. Some of DP's close friends, such as, Satyendranath Bose, Susobhan Sarkar, Girijapati Bhattacharya, Hirankumar Sanyal, Dilip-kumar Ray, and Hirendranath Mukherjee, contributed articles and book reviews to the journal as did DP's youngest brother Bimalaprosad Mukerji.

DP's writings in Bengali can be grouped under four heads: his creative works including the trilogy of novels, *Antahsila* (1935), *Abarta* (1937), and *Mohana* (1943) and his volume of short stories, *Realist* (1933); his correspondence with Rabindranath Tagore on music and allied topics collected together in the volume *Sur O Sangati* (1935), and his other writings on music including the book *Katha O Sur* (1938); his free-wheeling reflections and reminiscences written in the form of a diary in two volumes, *Mone Elo* (1956) and *Jhilimili* (1965, Preface 1961); his essays on social and cultural issues including *Amra O Tanhara* (1931), a volume of dialogic discussions, several collections such as *Chintayasi* (1933) and *Baktabya* (1957) and other essays.

This is not the place for an extensive critique of DP's creative writings which have received due attention from scholars and critics of Bengali literature. It may be interesting however for his non-Bengali readers to know that the titles of his three novels, *Antahsila* (Subterranean), *Abarta* (Eddy), and *Mohana* (Estuary), all have reference to a stream and that it has generally been assumed that DP adopted in his trilogy the stream of consciousness technique variously employed by Marcel Proust, James Joyce, and Virginia Woolf in their fiction. However, in his Preface to the last novel *Mohana*, DP wrote that on rereading the entire trilogy he found more of evolution and less of a stream. The evolution involves the two principal characters, Khagen-babu and Romola, and comes about through their interior monologues as well as their dialogues. The novels are deeply thought-provoking and take us towards the one belief that informed all of DP's writings, both creative and academic, whether in Bengali or in English—and that is—a belief in the

Personality—its evolution within and its connection with the surrounding community. The hero Khagenbabu is an urbane intellectual, deeply intro-spective and self-analytical. His double quest for the meaning of life and his own destiny culminates, after many experiences, in an engagement with society and a commitment to action in support of industrial workers. From an individual he becomes a person. A striking aspect of the trilogy, especially of the first two novels, is the author's representation of the character of Romola. DP was not known to have any feminist leanings; in fact his writings were strewn with sardonic and often negative comments about women. Yet, when it came to the heroine of his novels, he unfolded the person in all her complexity of intellect, emotion and feminine sensibility within this woman. The term *purusha* normally refers to the male person. But DP expli-citly states at the beginning of his essay 'For Humanism: Against Individual-ism' that the *purusha* appropriate to the spirit of the age is not the *purusha* of Sankhya philosophy. That is, among other implications, he did not quite have in mind the male principle in the male/female duality of *purusha* and *prakriti*. Could it be then that the *purusha* of DP's *purushavada* was not exclusively the male *purusha* but, as in Sanskrit grammar, the gender neutral 'person'? Romola is independent and non-conformist, which may have been regarded as masculine traits in the 1930s when the book appeared, but she is undoubtedly a woman in all her self-expression, in her desires and in her resentments. The final image we have of her—not as a social person but as a socialite estranged from the socially committed Khagenbabu—is an unfortu-nate but inevitable surrender to patriarchy. When the man in her life grows out of the relationship, she is left rudderless despite all her previous independ-ence. Thus Romola in *Mohana* cannot evolve adequately as a person; her society does not allow her to do so.

DP's book of short stories *Realist*, that had appeared earlier in 1933, elicited an extended response from Rabindranath Tagore which was printed in *Parichay* (April–May 1934). Here is an extract in my translation:

> Needless to say, man is not merely an animal, and this is why the supra-natural has manifested itself within the natural in man's nature—that literat-ure in which this duality does not find expression is without credibility and is also unable to give pleasure. . . . I am trying to say in my exposition what you have conveyed beguilingly through your stories. There is a roar of mocking laughter in your naming the book Realist. You have brought out in your stories the oddity and incongruity of pure and simple realism. A man can by nature be a villain, but when he girds his loins to be a realist, he becomes unnatural. That is, he becomes unreal. You have repeatedly

shown in your stories that those who cultivate realism as an ideal are
devoted really to a pose. They cannot forget for a moment that they are
realists nor do they let others forget it. They engage in image mongering.

DP was possibly the only person with whom Rabindranath co-authored
a book. The correspondence between them on the subject of music was
published as a book, *Sur O Sangati*. DP's sociological approach to music is
apparent in the opening sentence of *Indian Music: an Introduction* (1945,
2002): 'Indian music, being music, is just an arrangement of sounds; being
Indian it is certainly a product of Indian History.' DP was well versed in the
theory and rules of Indian classical music on which he held discussions with
Pandit Bhatkhande and Pandit Srikrishna Ratanjankar, and had heard most
of the renowned classical musicians of his time perform in public as well as
in small informal gatherings. His knowledge and understanding of Indian
classical music are acknowledged by scholars of the subject even today. But
DP was not such a classicist as to be indifferent to the newer and lighter
forms of music especially when it came to compositions in his mother tongue.
The music of Rabindranath delighted him and his personal closeness to
Tagore and Atulprasad Sen, second in his time only to Tagore as a song
writer and composer, inspired him to extend the theme of his discourse on
music. DP's second book on music *Katha O Sur* (1938) explores the relationship between words and melody in Bengali songs but with an eye to history
and viewing Bengali music as a course flowing from the mainstream of
Indian classical music, itself fed by many waters. The volume *Baktabya*
from which the essays translated in this volume have been selected also
contains two essays on music. These Bengali writings should be read along
with the two English works *Indian Music: an Introduction* and *Tagore: a
Study* (1943, 2001) for a comprehensive idea of DP's analytical evaluation
of historical and contemporary trends in Indian music.

In the last phase of his life when he was terminally ill, DP decided to
write down some of the thoughts arising out of his vast reading, his meetings
with a vast circle of acquaintances, and his engagement with the vast pano-
rama of life. In *Mone Elo* and *Jhilimili* we catch a glimpse of the man who
made a mark on all who knew him, old and young, with the sharpness of
his intellect, the range of his knowledge, the extent of his interests and the
lustre of his language. His entire life had been a dialogue—with his mentors,
his friends and equals, and with his students. Here we find him in dialogue
with himself. The result, as with his other dialogues, was enlightening for
himself and for others. He knew, though, that his writings would be read
and liked only by a few.

We turn now to our main concern in this book, DP's writings on social issues. The first to appear among these was *Amra O Tanhara* (We and They) collected together and published in 1931. The essays are in the form of dialogues where 'We' or 'I' stands for the intellectuals within the middle class while 'They' are the representatives of the less educated section of the middle class, the common white collar employees, who bring into play a different, if not entirely opposite, point of view. Thus, we have a set of reasoned-out arguments on one side, and a kind of 'common sense' position on the other. The issues debated include nationalism, revolution, music, literature, psychology, and the relationship between the sexes. The cut and thrust between scientific and rational thinking on the one hand and practical human values on the other is made attractive by wit, irony, and the genuine good humour of the interlocutors. However, it was not always possible for the author to retain the separate identities. In fact, DP gives the show away in his Preface to the second edition, published twenty-five years later: 'All thinking is dialogue between You and Me, or between ego and super-ego.' Much of the debate took place in DP's own mind, between two aspects of his own entity, and the dialogues reveal how much each needs the other to make up a whole.

DP's preoccupation with scientific and philosophic truth, with society and civilization, with literature and Rabindranath continues in his second book of essays titled *Chintayasi* (Reflect!). The dedication to Shri Pramatha Chowdhury is DP's acknowledgement of his debt to his preceptor in the art and craft of criticism. A notable essay in this collection is 'Normal', a scathing indictment of the search for normality in general, and of the so-called scientific basis of the statistical average in particular. In its application to politics the standard becomes a frightful thing. In the concluding lines of this essay written in 1925/26, DP might have anticipated the logic adopted by the National Socialists in Germany and others of their kind: 'Earlier we had only been counting heads, but now the group is firmly established with the discovery that it has a mind. A leader of that group is telling us to surrender ourselves to the collective mind—after a few days he will surely tell us that the collective mind is the only mind. But this he has not dared to do as yet. At present he is indicating only the way in which to make the self-surrender. The way is discipline, that is, German drill.'

Baktabya, which can be loosely translated as 'Statements', was published in 1957 though the essays were written much earlier. Eight of the essays that appeared in this book have been translated and presented here. Other essays that deal with cultural issues, mostly devoted to different aspects of Tagore's work, have not been translated.

In several essays in the present collection, DP confronts the dominant force of modern history, individualism, and points out its destructive potential. A Western concept, the 'individual' was born as a consequence of Renaissance humanism, one of the components of which was daring individual enterprise for the sake of profit. The 'man' of humanism became an 'individual' under the pressure of capitalism. The sense of community was lost and the decline of European culture began in the Renaissance itself [Chapter 1]. The second image of modern Western humanism was Rousseau's 'noble savage'. A romantic rebellion against the rigid norms of the feudal social order, Rousseau's doctrine envisaged such progressive ideals as democracy and a new system of education. As a forerunner of the French Revolution, Rousseau produced ideas which would become powerful instruments of social change. However, Rousseau's idea of romantic individual freedom and the goodness of the primitive natural state of man held seeds not of change but of disintegration. His noble savage culminated in the nihilist–anarchist of nineteenth and twentieth-century Europe and in the fascism of Hitler [Chapter 2]. Nurtured by humanism, the 'individual' became a full-blown concept in the age of capitalism in England. It became an abstraction and man became separated from the totality of nature. Marxism countered the force of individualism, seeing it as allied to capitalism, by relating to the individual being not directly but through a human community. The profiteering individual pursuing his lonely path of self-aggrandizement and the nameless individuals who get crushed in the process of creating profit for him are both alienated from their true natures. Marxism restores humanity to man [Chapter 4]. As to liberalism, the other concomitant of capitalism, its true nature becomes abundantly clear with time. The individual liberty that was championed was not for everybody but for the propertied class [Chapter 7]. With the sense of community lost, nationalism rushed in to fill the vacuum. The Renaissance saw the formation of nation states, which desired to extend their power just as individuals desire to increase their gain. National interest then clashed with individual self-interest and the collective sought to restrain the individual. In protest, the individual responded by seeking to obtain control of the state. Both the action and the reaction imperilled democracy [Chapter 1].

A powerful force in the history of humanity of all times has been faith and DP engages seriously with the question of faith. He considers the position of eminent Western thinkers such as Weber and Tawney who have observed that faith in God has acted as inducement to hard work. DP notes, however, that although the ascetic ideal was historically associated with the rise of capitalism, as capitalism developed, the doctrine of individual freedom and the business attitude undermined faith [Chapter 1]. Also, having no reason to be eurocentric, he looks eastward and finds that faith alone was not responsible for the spread of Islam. His familiarity with contemporary research in the area revealed to him the historical factors behind the spread of Islam and suggested to him the ingredients of faith in the first age of Islam. Nor was religious faith at the root of the glorious ages of Indian history. However, DP writes with some concern a year after Partition, India and Pakistan both had religion at their inception. Pakistan was established as a theocratic state. India took the way of secularism but with *Ramarajya* on its lips. The great irony is that Gandhi's faith was many times greater than Jinnah's, yet India stood to lose while Pakistan gained. Given the adverse effect of religion on the subcontinent, its efficacy is in question. Thus, if ever there was a connection between faith in God and human advancement, it is unlikely that this can be recovered in the modern age [Chapter 1]. Nevertheless, faith is needed, but faith in man. The question is, which kind of faith in man should guide us, since there are many brands of it. Not Renaissance humanism, surely, for it has led to the disintegration of European culture [Chapter 1]. Nor should it be a pursuit of Gandhi's ideal man who is of the same breed as the noble savage. It is alarming that two of the main tenets of European anarchists, descendants of Rousseau's noble savage, as mentioned earlier, can be found in Gandhi's thought, namely, decentralization and federalism. The difference is that Gandhi's concept of the ideal man and his conduct was based on faith in God while Rousseau had kept God apart from the active public life. Gandhi's faith in God was a source of strength for him in practical life, but as God cannot bridge the gap between ideal truth and practical reality, Gandhian thought has its inherent defect. Thus Gandhi's trust in man was betrayed. When control was lifted as he had wished, the players in the white market outdid those in the black market in their greed [Chapter 2]. The positivism of Comte and Harrison and the scientific humanism of Julian Huxley cannot provide the answer either, for they invariably postulate a religion devoid of man [Chapter 2]. DP submits that in the new society of independent India faith in man can only mean faith in the *purusha* or the human personality in evolution, unfettered yet related to its social matrix [Chapters 2 and 3].

As DP surveys the situation in India before independence he discerns three features of India's psychological history: the use of traditional philosophic and religious nomenclature, the patriotism of an oppressed nation, and liberalism learnt from the British masters. Each of these features is exploited in turn by the Brahmin class, the Congress, and the educated members of society in a 'secret conspiracy.' Gandhi's religion with all its concern for the untouchables, leaves the caste system intact, and the upper castes continue to be at the top of the social hierarchy. The wealthy class has come forward to be of service to the nation symbolized by the Congress but, in its greater regard for itself, has succeeded in enlisting the service of the Congress in advancing its own agenda. As to those belonging to the educated class, they are puppets of a foreign ideology and betrayers of the hopes of their own people. All this compounded with the consequences of imperialist domination and monopolistic trade has created a complex situation [Chapter 7]. DP points out how important it is to recognize that the strongest current in modern Indian history is capitalism's exploitation of the colonies. The treaty of Versailles was an understanding reached between the warring and wealthy countries of the West. It was a pact to carve up the rest of the world—portions of Asia and Africa that each would get to further their economic gains. Competition between the rich has led to innovations in scientific methods of production. Science is thus harnessed for the benefit of the wealthy, to reduce loss and increase profit for them with workers remaining where they are. If competition is one aspect of market economy, forming alliances to keep afloat is another. Many social scientists speak in terms of the world becoming one. DP sees global alliances as another name for the establishment of a global empire. He cautions Indian intellectuals that the present condition of India cannot be understood unless it is located in this context [Chapters 6 and 7]. The fact that the wealthy class in the colonies has become patriotic is, as stated above, not an unmixed blessing; its good side must also be acknowledged which is the rise in nationalism and an attendant sense of responsibility. This also provides a link between India and the world for nationalism is a strong force in Europe too. The lesser colonial powers have turned their attention to their own countries, concentrating on unification, removal of tariffs for free movement of goods, and building up of infrastructure. The wealthy in India rallying behind the national flag could well bring about similar advantages for their own homeland [Chapter 7]. DP surveys the scene just after independence once again. The British had left behind a wreck. The administration was in a shambles and the hatred between Hindus and Muslims was enervating the country. Continuing feudal oppression and capitalist exploitation of the common people raises the question: independence for whom? In the sphere of economics, the government in collusion with the Indian business class was engaged in mystification, for the much vaunted division of assets really amounted to nothing but capital accumulation in the hands of a few powerful private individuals. In such a situation DP calls upon Indian economists and intellectuals to use their analytical tools to understand the reality which is that the rich are literally capitalizing confusion in order to get richer [Chapter 5].

One of the common strands of the essays presented here is the conviction of the overwhelming importance of history as a guide to the present and the future. In the nascent stage of an independent modern India, DP says, the vision that must inform all activity is that a new social structure stands not only on changed perceptions but also on hard work [Chapter 1]. This is the first lesson of history and is related to the second, for history's understanding of change suggests that philosophy too is not eternal and fixed but suited to an age. Thus, the new social philosophy of new India must enunciate its first resolve, which is diligence and experience working hand in hand with experimentation [Chapter 2]. The dialectical functioning of society is also revealed by history as Marx perceived it. DP favours the historical materialism of Marxism because it enables us to see the dynamics of the social process [Chapter 4]. But analytical thinking does not stop at mere assertions, it looks at indicators. Thus DP advocates a perusal of the causes and consequences of the major civil wars in the history of the world. If history is to act as a guide, it is important to know the aspirations as well as inherent weaknesses of the parties in conflict. An understanding of the causes of fraternal strife in America, Spain and China along with the spectacle of devastation caused by such internecine wars can bring about change in the existing attitudes of a people. The disunited Indian left could draw a lesson from the history of Germany where the Communist Party and the Social Democrats, ranged against each other, left the field clear for Hitler [Chapter 5]. Perhaps the most important argument regarding the primacy of history is the one constant factor found to be present throughout man's life on earth, namely his struggle for survival within a given environment and his attempt to live a better life. This is also the reason why man found it necessary to form a society in the first place. History takes note of the various stages of man's struggle for survival and thus maps the varying equations between science and society, for science is man's chief instrument of survival [Chapter 6].

If DP tells us about the significance of history in respect of both knowledge and action, he also writes about how to engage with history and how not to. First of all, a concept of history needs to be developed. Of the several constructions of history that exist, DP dismisses the imaginative for being vague, the utopian for its unrealistic loss of contact with time and the supernatural for excluding man from its scheme, or, at any rate, for making the great majority of men and women irrelevant for its devised purpose. The only valid interpretation of history is a scientific one in which events are externalized and concretized; their sequence and interrelation are examined [Chapter 6]. Events, moreover, must be analysed. We must, for instance, be aware of the changing forms of Western colonialism, of the vestiges of feudalism which linger on, of the reasons behind administrative failure, of the grounds of communal hatred. The communal situation must be viewed from the perspective of the large segment of Muslim peasant and workers who are 'unlettered, exploited and subjugated.' Any other kind of attitude such as, for instance, the solicitude of the slogan 'Muslim mass contact', is spurious and in the long run harmful [Chapter 5]. But who will write this balanced, analytical history of India? DP laments the fact that the educated class in India has stepped out of history. It follows the model of the English liberal blindly. No one writes social history or the history of the common people based on causality and showing how the social organization changes at critical moments of history to ensure the survival of society. Economists too are unsure of themselves. On the one hand they espouse the cause of agriculture and cottage industry; on the other hand, as liberals they advocate free trade, forgetting that the concept of free trade is related to the industrialism of the West. Our curriculum does not include the history of the Balkans or Russia,[1] countries with an agricultural economy. It is an anomalous situation that born in the twentieth century, the Indian intellectual has adopted the ideology of liberalism evolved in the 'Age of Enlightenment' in eighteenth century Europe. He has uncritically adopted a model without examining whether it is relevant or suited to Indian society [Chapter 7]. In the last of his three historical essays, however, DP sounds a positive note as he makes the hopeful proposition that placing faith in history it is possible to bring about social change and progress. Here he outlines the course for the social historian who must first of all be imbued with moral judgment and a code of values. With the understanding that progress through conflict is the law of the universe, the social historian must consciously use it in his narrative to encourage social change and the removal of class differences. The Marxist perspective is clearly discernible in the assertion that not only is this the historian's duty to society as a conglomerate but that it will liberate every person living in society 'for it is due to class difference that man is unable to attain full humanity' [Chapter 8].

At the hour of independence, profoundly disheartened by the turn of events, DP chose to nourish his vision of the future with the faith he had always advocated, faith in humanity and faith in history. He makes two suggestions, one requiring collective effort and the other invoking the singular

---

[1] This was the case at the time DP wrote these essays.

being within every person. Censuring the Communist Party for its mistimed criticism of the Congress and Gandhi, DP nevertheless reposes trust in the left parties. These parties must move closer to the working class and make common cause with it. They must fulfil their historical role by coming together and remaining united. DP hopes that this will come about under pressure from workers and peasants. As to arousing the awareness of the working class, he sees this clearly as the responsibility of intellectuals. Economists in particular must have contact with the masses, clear up their confusions and educate them. Working in tandem, intellectuals and a united left with its social orientation can provide a direction for independent India [Chapters 1 and 5]. DP's prescription for man in the new society is that he must be a *purusha* or a 'person', related to and integrated with society as opposed to an individual alienated from society. Every human being evolves within a social habitat, which comprises the primary circle of biological ties and several successive secondary circles. After his growth in the first necessary phase of nurture, man tries to free himself from animal ties, not for the sake of individual freedom but to build and participate in other groups with new rules and regulations. This is how the personality is formed as it emerges, in DP's metaphor, like a silkworm cutting through its own cocoon. Taking the analogy further we can say that perhaps DP was arguing that just as a natural organism flourishes in and evolves out of a favourable environment, so does a person impelled by conscious action open up possibilities of transition. Men and women conscious of their situation in a historical process can, in association with other members of the community, apply a set of theoretical tools for an action programme that seeks to achieve certain collective goals. In the process such creative activity reinforces the theoretical and practical instruments of the actors in a community in bringing about the desired change. This is very similar to the sense in which the term 'praxis' is used in Marxist discourse. In this view of the person in society, determinism is limited, as is individual freedom. While the individual whose concept of truth is based on the either/or logic finds the limits bewildering, the *purusha* negotiates them confidently, resolving contradictions between rights and responsibilities, between tradition and experiment. In his brief exposition of the theory of personalism, DP emphasizes the importance of keeping the class structure open. Only then will the democratic principle underlying the theory be fully realized [Chapters 2, 3, and 4].

The concept of the *purusha* is central to DP's proposition for a new philosophy for modern India. As it is based on faith in man, this theory of personalism can be called a kind of humanism though it is different from earlier forms of humanism. DP presents his theory of the new humanism briefly but systematically. He first demonstrates, as discussed earlier, how the known varieties of humanism have all failed either by dint of some basic flaw or by suffering distortion at the hands of individuals who have used it to further their own wealth, power, or theoretical doctrine. This prepares the ground for first positing and then formulating a new theory of humanism that is proffered in the idea of *purushavada*. In choosing an Indian name DP further signifies his rejection of most Western brands of humanism. He finds merit in the concept of human nature in Indian society—both Hindu and Muslim— that, despite all disruptive and divisive forces, is true to the bond between human beings and their surrounding community. The freedom or independence of the individual is not at such a premium yet in India as to turn society into a mass of discrete, rootless beings. But while Indian society is better than its counterparts in Europe in providing a good foundation for humanism, it does have its limitations which must be transcended. The greatest drawback of Indian society is its hide-bound class structure. This is where DP turns to another strand of Western thought, namely Marxism. For him, Marxism has the advantage of applying not just to conditions of European countries in a particular age but to other lands and times as well because it addresses itself to the problem of all class-ridden societies. DP considers Marxism to be the best form of humanism to have emerged from the West, for it is not the unconnected individual being that is at the centre of Marxism but man as part of a larger humanity. Marxism with its understanding of the dynamics of the social process, its analysis of class conflict, and its inclusive view of life that yet appreciates the specificity of human action can be of help in overcoming the imperfections of India's social philosophy as it has evolved over the ages. Thus, DP redefines humanism by bringing Marxism into alliance with Indian values. His fusion of the two produces his vision of the *purusha,* a person who is integrated, confident, and industrious and whose progress is inevitably linked with the development of the ambient society.

SROBONA MUNSHI

PART ONE

REFLECTIONS ON HUMANISM

1

Faith in Man

Many things are needed in the new India that has emerged. The need for various new material goods is on everybody's lips. This is natural and in keeping with societal norms. New eagerness and even new points of view are also being mentioned but less often. We did not think of what would happen after getting rid of the British. Those who did relied more on the unspoiled, unaffected, primordial and innate energy of the nation than on reflection and logic. This is why they were unable to unfold before the public any image of the future India; this too is natural but contrary to the demands of society. The image envisaged by Mahatmaji did, without doubt, capture momentarily the fancy of a few, if not of the common people at large—but the black cloud lurking near soon enveloped it. Many books have been written about it, many programmes have been initiated according to it, many a good and great man has been influenced by it; nevertheless, for many reasons, the country as a whole has remained indifferent to it. It is not impossible to cast or to secure votes on the strength of devotion, but so long as the people have not turned into a band of sycophants, the efficacy of devotional chanting is bound to be false and short-lived. This is where the need arises for Leftist parties. However, there is very little reflection on the nature of the Leftist movement even now in this country. Many of us are acquainted with the writings of Marx and of foreign Marxists; we have created many variants of socialist parties, we are reading and writing articles in the mother tongue; but the amount of mental agility, depth and analysis that is required to manifest the republican image of India to its people is hardly to be found. Literature with communist leanings has the widest

SROBONA MUNSHI, formerly of the Department of English, University of Calcutta, has translated 'Faith in Man' (originally titled 'Nabya Samajdarshaner Bhumika 1' or 'The Role of the New Social Philosophy 1', written in 1948–49).

circulation; but in spite of some new facts thrown in, its purport is obscured by the excess of adulation; its thinking is mechanical. Socialist literature has begun to be publicized but apart from the writings of Manabendranath Roy, other discussions are not in evidence. Gandhian socialism has seized this moment to evolve. Perhaps this is nothing but a sign of opportunism. Gandhians have understood the wisdom of adopting the term socialism; and many individuals angry and dissatisfied with the Congress [Party] are realizing that even while moving away from the policy of the Congress Party it would be unwise to drop the name of Gandhiji. But the fundamental differences between Gandhism and socialism have not as yet been analysed, there is only bickering about the nomenclature. And so it seems that the greatest need of the new India is for a new philosophy.

Even after the task of creating a metaphysics is entrusted to specialists, it is seen that bringing about a change in the perception of the masses is not entirely impossible. Indeed, it is the present situation that is conducive to change. The uranium age is knocking at the door of the iron-and-steel age, India's inherent power is being put to the test, the agrarian life is rapidly losing ground to mechanical civilization, feudal rule is dying out, capitalism is alive and vigorous, the power of the old social order has diminished and the new social order is casting its reflection on the public mind. Of course, examples of missed opportunities are strewn all over the pages of history. Many nations, oblivious to the call of circumstances, have remained immersed in eternal stupor. Again, for many nations, the faint note of a slim chance has provided sufficient inspiration. But since it is not desirable for the new India to be perplexed by a profusion of historical instances or to engage in the luxury of dispassionate meditation with their help, there is no other alternative for it but to consciously utilize all social opportunities. Otherwise India will only dream of independence and then turn over on its side in sleep. Thus wide experience must be based on hard work—this is the first resolve of the new social philosophy. This is not the place to examine the many manifestations of industriousness in the history of Western philosophy. Let it suffice to mention two of its basic principles: the experiential and the experimental. Action according to the *Sruti* and the *Smriti* has more to do with carrying out orders than with enterprise and self-reliance. However, for a variety of reasons a new mode of action swiftly takes on a routine and customary aspect, which is why the spirit of inquiry must be constantly kept alive. Fortunately, aversion to inquiry is decreasing with the spread of science. On the other hand, society has become so complex that the impetus to work provided by old-world idealism is not enough. Everybody knows that the spirit of self-sacrifice has become weaker with the attainment of independence. The voluntary freedom fighter is now an employee.

Idealism is based on faith in God. Whether that faith is still intact or not is subject to proof. One cannot take a gallup poll on this. If it is claimed that fewer people go to church today then this can be countered with the example of Russians marching towards the church. Faith in God is said to persist in Catholic Europe, Asia and Latin America. The matter cannot be settled by numbers. It can be measured only by the principal and dominant current of activity in a society. Belief in such activity is so prevalent that it seems to be like faith in God. Just so much, if not more, of singlemindedness and self-denial can be seen in the practice of the affluent class today as the intense faith that we know was present in the practice of the medieval saints, ascetics, and monks and friars. Asceticism is one of the leading principles and historical grounds of capitalism. In the first stage [of capitalism] the difference between the two faiths is not apparent because the affluent are pious both as private individuals and in their observance of rituals. In course of time as faith becomes weaker, acts of bounty and charity become manifold. Thereafter, the building of infirmaries for cattle (pinjrapols), hospitals for women and temples cannot contain the piety and faith spills over to the gurus and holy men, and even later to conservative and royalist groups and even to research associations. Centred around Gandhi, making use of his name and thus consolidating capitalism may be a new phenomenon in our country but elsewhere the method has long been employed. This is precisely how capitalism has developed in Europe; many instances of which have been recovered from the history of the late middle ages by such scholars as Weber and Tawney among others. But two internal conflicts remain unresolved. The Reformation that visited Europe after the Renaissance had as its main achievement individual liberty. Further back in time, the system of accounting that was devised to facilitate business in the middle phase of the medieval age resulted in what Sombart has called the rational outlook. Both of these are inimical to old forms of religious faith. Because the British ruined our trade, as well as for a few other reasons—primarily that of the peculiarity of the system of education—the rational outlook did not spread among us, nor did business morality. There is, however, an intimate connection between a kind of Protestant individual freedom with its concomitant reformist temper and Indian capitalism, which is most evident in the state of Bombay. Thus belief in the doctrine of individual freedom is still the most active belief among capitalists in this country. And this is why its anger with the current of thought inherent in socialism springs from its own creed. Needless to say, the kind of religion which helps the cause of capitalism and the rise and spread of the doctrine of individual freedom is bound to undergo a gradual weakening of faith in God. Whatever little remains also disappears as it faces the threat of the rationalistic temper. In the end there is only the business attitude that prevails; that is, let the state be run by business-men and according to the rules and practices that ensure the augmentation of business. Mahatmaji and Calvin had wanted both the state and business enterprise to be infused with piety, spirituality and morality; their disciples have, in their name, slowly established the state and even religion as instru-ments of business. Of course, faith survived; only the object of faith changed. There used to be heaven, virtue and appreciation of merit; there was God; there are now this world, happiness, self-confidence, worship of numbers, crores for the sake of crores. Mahatmaji was the last God-fearing leader not just in India but in all the world except Africa and perhaps Central Asia and Pakistan. Thus faith in God cannot be the basis of a suitable social philosophy for modern times. It will be valid, I think, only for individuals.

There is an opposition between the first proposition and the second mentioned above. Faith in God is one of the mainsprings of proclivity to action. Many say that the spread of Islam is due to this. It is also at the root of the success of many who have dedicated themselves to active life. We all know of the examples of Mahatmaji, Vivekananda, Rabindranath and others. But on analysis, the matter does not appear to be very simple. It is harsh and rude to discuss personal lives, for many of us are acquainted with quite a few successful individuals who have climbed to the top of the society, of their profession and service, by mixing devotion with appeasement of their powerful superiors. The formula for a successful life is flattery + profi-ciency + faith in God. True faith in God, though, leads man to renunciation, or else it makes him inert, confined to his old familiar place. On reading the new research work on the spread of Islam it seems that the factors responsible for it are trade and commerce of the Arabs, the feebleness of the conquered nations and the comparative backwardness of the Middle East, Central Asia and North Africa at that time. Besides, the faith of the first age of Islam was somewhat different and cannot be compared with the faith of Gandhiji or Rabindranath. The ingredients of that faith were partly fear, partly the intense desire to return to the ancestral centre of power, and partly a millennial hope. In particular there were such socially oriented notions as the advanced nature of Islam compared to idolatrous faiths and its greater capacity to establish peace. The God of a prophetic religion exacts one kind of faith from human beings, the God of a revealed religion exacts another kind. This seems to be true also when one considers the activities of Jesus Christ and Saint Paul. If the Hindu religion is seen as founded on the *Veda*s then a God has to be discovered to account for the spread of the Aryan civilization. Asoka was a Buddhist but the spread of Buddhism was certainly not due to faith in God. There is no evidence to suggest that faith was responsible for such glorious ages in Indian history as the Gupta empire or the kingdom of Harshavardhana. The advent of God possibly, nay certainly, exerted an elevating influence on the practice of religion; but can it be said that it brought about wealth of knowledge and action among the Hindu people? Who can loudly proclaim that the Vaishnava philosophy with its emphasis on faith is superior to *Sankhya*, the *Vedanta* and *Nyaya*? Thus, if ever there was a connection between faith in God and industriousness, this cannot be recovered in the modern age.

Yes, at the inception of Pakistan, religion certainly had a role to play, but the British were no less responsible. Similarly, in independent India too there is an association between the state and religion along with some unintended help from the British. At the very moment the Indian government of our plans was to become a secular one, the term *Ramarajya* was heard. And Rama *was* God—not a piece of Divinity, but the Whole. So, what it all amounts to is this: independent India has at its origin faith in God, so does Pakistan. But while one suffered a loss, the other stood to gain, though Mahatmaji's faith was many times greater than Jinnah's. It is unlikely that a faith which brings about an adverse result would be effective in the present age.

Faith, however, is urgently needed. There are socially prescribed ways of increasing the desire for faith, but that is not the subject of this essay. The primary question is, faith in what? Of course, it has to be faith in man. History shows us that there are many faces of faith in man (of the religion of man, the humane) and of them there are three which are most lustrous. There are three components in the humanism of the Renaissance: the experimentalism of the Greeks, personal daring for the sake of profit resulting from expansion of trade, and the legacy of Christian civilization. The opposition between the second and the third components was resolved by the Reformation, which gave its verdict in favour of the second. Consequently, the individual was born in Europe. Whether this consequence was good or bad is well known to us. What we understand by European culture began to decline from the time of the Renaissance itself. The basis of culture is not the individual but the community or *samaj* (society) as Hindus call it. When the sense of community is lost, the need for nationalism arises to fill up the empty space. Just as an individual is one, so too a nation is one; just as an individual is adventurous for the sake of gain, so too is a nation desirous of extending its power. Nation gives rise to the national state, and even as this is in the making, the individual is sought to be restrained—for such is the nature of the collective. The individual protests in the name of freedom by seeking to obtain control of the state. This is why we encounter the phenomenon of mercantilism immediately prior to the time that the idea of democracy gained currency. The strain of the same tune has pierced the voice of the people and is making itself heard in the menacing roar of governments today. Such is the plight of Renaissance humanism!

2

Further Thoughts on Faith in Man

The second known form of humanism was the creation of Rousseau. The man of his imagination was basically good. In the beginning of society man was simple, straight, liberal and noble; but due to the insistence of some selfish individuals and the need for money society was formed and since then began all sorts of trouble. According to Rousseau, the return of man to his primitive natural state was not only desirable but possible too. That is why he recommended democracy and a new system of education. In those days of feudalism, romantic individual freedom was the only form of protest against the strict rules of social order. From this angle alone he was the forerunner of the French Revolution. But just this statement is not enough. He was the bearer of the trend of disintegration of European civilization and community from the period of the Renaissance–Reformation. Till the seventeenth century, there was a connection between man and the supernatural—the life of mystics, the symbols used in poetry and the rise of various secret religious sects are proof of this. But in the eighteenth century, the connection became loose, according to some, owing to the blessings of science. This is true to some extent: it becomes apparent when the faith of the earlier scientists like Newton, Pascal and others is compared with that of the scientists of the later half of the eighteenth century. Probably there was another belief behind the spread of experiment-based science. The revolt that raised its head against mercantilism in the mid-eighteenth century had its philosophical basis in the idealism, not of Berkeley, but of Locke and others. The main purport of this idealism is individual freedom—of course in accordance with

SANJUKTA DASGUPTA, Professor, Department of English, University of Calcutta, has translated 'Further Thoughts on Faith in Man' (originally titled 'Nabya Samajdarshaner Bhumika 2' or 'The Role of the New Social Philosophy 2', written in 1948–49).

the English constitution. 'English' because it was first in England that the feudal states were abolished and class based states evolved in the name of individual freedom. The imaginary man of English idealism is neither 'noble' nor 'savage', but 'nobleman'. Later he came to be known as John Halifax, the gentleman. But in Europe the notion of gentleman is not found. So the heroes of Jules Verne, Conrad are Englishmen. The reason for this being: after the abolition of the elite class in Europe, no middle class had evolved which, by virtue of its control over the country's state machinery, could convert the noble savage imagined by Rousseau into a gentleman. The gentleman of England was the backbone of English society; their civic and political consciousness kept the state alive; their voluntary service lessened the pressure on the state and contained and obstructed the movement towards democracy. But in Europe, the ideal of the noble savage or that of the rural peasant continued to survive due to the absence or comparatively lesser influence of the middle class. The examples of the social outlook of Lord Shaftesbury on the one hand and on the other of Bakunin and Kropotkin as the representatives of the elite class are enough. The European terroristic nihilist and Hitler–Ludendorff are the offspring of Rousseau's 'noble savage'. The anarchism and fascism of the present are like two cousins. Now we have to consider to what extent we shall or can accept this type of humanism.

The ideal man of Gandhian Society is of the same breed as the 'noble savage'. Mahatma Gandhi had trust in the innate goodness of man. The truth in the *satyagraha* approved by him is God but desire is inherent in man. Awakening the innate simple and good inclinations of man was the main theme of his grand movement and the real purpose in ascertaining the true relationship between Hindu and Muslim, upper and lower caste, wealthy and working class, king and servant. He wanted from every man, every Indian the natural simplicity of the 'savage'. The sign of this conviction was evident in his imagined and approved social organization. The social organization of European anarchists had two main doctrines—'decentralization' and 'federalism'. The first was the reaction of the Industrial period and the second of the nineteenth century state system. We know that the planned society of Gandhi was to be founded on the decentralized economy. Although his concept of federalism was not clear in his writings, he was so opposed to centralization that we might roughly call him a kind of federalist. Needless to say, his federalism was not of the Jefferson type. His trust in cooperative society was his other similarity with the anarchists. It was not of the English type, but like the panchayat society of our country or the Russian 'Mir' society of Kropotkin's liking. This cooperative society was also suitable for the 'noble savage'. (Of course, Saratchandra, a Gandhi follower, had different ideas regarding the future of rural society and panchayat). Perhaps further similarities cannot be found. The differences are now demanding attention.

The 'morality' of Blanqui, Bakunin, Kropotkin, etc. (Sorel is an anarchist of a different kind) is very clear. But the Gandhian concept of right conduct is absolutely different as it is based on faith in God. Rousseau and Voltaire also believed in God; but they kept Him apart from the social life and the practical world, i.e. the public domain. The duality of deism was not there in Gandhiji's views. The result of this was good for himself and for his close followers too. It is God who protects him. At the same time Hindu society also has to be considered. No such pure totalitarian, regimented society exists in the whole world. Here, the extent of control is from conception up to the sixth generation after death. Here the only free person is one who has conquered the fruits of work. In this society, 'anarchism' is obsolete and belief in the 'noble savage' is beyond belief. Planning is in keeping with the norms of this society. The notion of state was irrelevant all this time because we did not have one; it is now on the verge of being created. Till the time it is permanently formed, the 'anarchist' ideal has no social meaning. Although the industrial civilization has set in, its influence and spread are not of such extent that opposition to it can be considered the philosophy of life. Although the sense of time, the most important virtue of industrial civilization, is not seen amongst the leaders of this country, still they, along with their dependants, are flying to Delhi and to England in airplanes. In this respect their humanity is still intact. Even now every Indian wants machines and is fascinated by the mechanical civilization. No villager or Hindu widow likes to go on a pilgrimage on foot. Although the farmers do not want to take to the tractors all of a sudden leaving their ploughs aside, it has not been ascertained whether it is due to the conservatism of the farmers or the incompetence of the Department of Agriculture. Moreover, are not the universities, educational institutions, laboratories, the best examples of mechanical civilization? That is, the demand for mechanical civilization is still immense. The Gandhian accepts this practical truth because of his belief in the 'noble savage' or the rural agriculturist: in other words and thoughts, because of his idealism. The gap between the two types of Truth—practical and ideal truth ('Nature as it is' and 'Nature as it should be' of medieval age) cannot be filled in this era by God, the Eternal Truth. This is true even in India, the proof being the new business agreement with the English in Gandhiji's lifetime despite his injunction, the black market in spite of his trust and entreaty, and, after his demise, such misuse of his blessing as 'decontrol'. The increase in the price of clothes in the last two or three months has loudly proclaimed the inherent defect in Gandhism. The 'nobility' of the 'noble savage' does not exist any longer, only the savagery remains. The sum and substance is: the man of Gandhian thought is not known to us, but the powerful men of the Gandhi era are controlling our lives. The main drawback of the idea of Rousseau or of the anarchists is that there is no touch of history in it. Therefore we want such humanism as is based on practical truth and historical facts. We do not want the kind of humanism that ends in nihilism—total negation, whose external expression is in the sound of the terrorist's gunshots or in Thoreau's exile, Tolstoy's escape, Nietzsche's superman, or in the strange, eccentric and non-conformist practice of ashram life. The new social philosophy is bound to be a little pessimistic.

A discussion of the humanism propounded by Comte, Harrison, Hume, Schiller, Julian Huxley, etc. is not as necessary here as it is in the textbooks. In reality, positivism and the succeeding scientific humanism are types of human religion devoid of man. Rabindranath has shown beautifully in his *Chaturanga* that religion cannot exist without both man and God. Even if we assume that Rabindranath did not understand it right, still, until state rule comes into the hands of the scientists, scientific humanism is meaningless. Rather, from what we see it appears that the scientists are eager to hand over the responsibility of state to others or to employers. Nowhere in the world does the scientific community control policy. I observed a strange thing the other day in the annual report and the appeal of the Indian Association of the Cultivation of Science in Bowbazar. The management is appealing to the affluent for fellowships. In the terms and conditions of this fellowship they have quoted a stipulation from the Mellon Endowment of America. One of the conditions is: the research paper will be published with the consent of the sponsor; that is if the sponsor does not give consent, no research paper can be published which might affect the sponsor's business interest, etc. The funny part is—these have been considered as parallel ideals. Those who are doing this are all patriots, renowned scientists, freedom lovers, respectful of research, believers in science and believers in the freedom of the scientists. Perhaps they think, let the money flow in and let science spread first, then it will be seen how powerful the rich are. Perhaps they have forgotten the present state of the patents. Perhaps they are overwhelmed by the fanfare of American money. But in America itself, Bell Telephone System suppressed 3400 unused patents for the sake of profit from monopoly business. This information is available in the 1937 official report of Federal Communications. Many such examples can be found in the essay titled 'The Key to the Ice Box', published in the 24 April 1948 edition of *The New Statesman*. For these reasons it seems that the scientists are not as yet fit for social thinking. It can even be said that it is unfair to expect any human virtue from scientists devoid of social sense. There is no difference between them and the idealist philosophers. Those who control the society can make fools of both these groups and keep them in servitude.

The argument has reached the point that philosophy is not eternal, but in accordance with the age, although every philosophy suitable for a particular age is eager to surpass the need of that age. If there is no response to the challenge of the new situation in India, it will die. Therefore the first resolve of the new philosophy is diligence, experience and experimentation. The philosophy that was prevalent so long, whatever name may be given to it, had its roots in faith in God. Nowadays belief in God is unable to infuse new life into society—although capitalism, the new force behind social change, is always eager to use it and assume its form for self-defence. But observing the activities of Indian capitalists it appears that they are inimical to real faith in God. Besides, our country is becoming secular. Faith, however, is needed. Only faith in man can take the place of faith in God. This faith too has different forms. The man of the Renaissance–Reformation age, under the pressure of capitalism, became an individual and from that day onwards European society ceased to exist. The ultimate consequences of the man of Rousseau's imagination are the nihilist-terrorist and Hitler. In scientific humanism there is no faith in man, there is only humanitarianism or an unreal object called 'common man', faith in which cannot inspire the society to evolve anew. Social consciousness does not as yet pervade the behaviour of the scientific community, at least not in our country. The question is then: which faith in man? Every Indian now realizes the defect of the trust in man conceived by Gandhi. He was a believer in the innate goodness of man and on the strength of this conviction he could do away with control. The result is white market, which is even more dangerous than black market. Therefore, the man of the new society cannot be a 'noble savage' or a scientist or an unevolved Deity. Man will have to be *purusha*. He cannot be an individual or a single entity. He has to be a person.

3

For Personalism: Against Individualism

The term *purusha* would not have had any special relevance had not individualism culminated in nihilism, that is, European social nihilism and the sheer worship of power, that is, terrorism. It is redundant to state that the term *purusha* appropriate for this age is not the same as the *purusha* of the *Sankhya* or that of the *Gita*. Yet there is a similarity between it and the *purushakara*, that is, relying on ones' own powers in order to liberate oneself voluntarily from the domination of nature and its cycle, and the cycle of *karma*. This is the reason why the use of the term *purusha* is especially appropriate. However, there is a lot of difference between individualism and personalism (*purushavada*). The first difference is that the individual is estranged from society and hence he becomes an enemy of society or a socially frustrated, alienated being. This sense of estrangement manifests itself in three conditions. The first is loneliness, which according to Durkheim leads to suicide and according to Erich Fromm, to fascism. The second is irresponsible criticism and anti-social behaviour, the proof of which is abundantly found in the city of Kolkata, in its lanes and bylanes, in trams and buses and in its tea shops and stores. The third is opposition for the sake of opposition, hoodwinking the law for the sake of hoodwinking it, disrespecting the police simply for the sake of disrespecting it, i.e., a general disregard for rules and regulations, and the habit of flouting the law. This condition is reflected in discounting planning, in the anarchy of capitalism and its international policies. The obscurity in poetry, the self-conceit of scientists and artists, the egoism of specialists and the self-satisfaction of social reformers

JHARNA SANYAL, Professor, Department of English, University of Calcutta, has translated 'For Personalism: Against Individualism' (originally titled 'Nabya Samajdarshaner Pratijna' or 'A Proposition for a New Social Philosophy', written in 1948–49).

are all manifestations of the contradiction that is inherent in individualism. The either/or in logic originates from this. There is no place here to enumerate how much damage this has caused to science and other branches of knowledge. In practical affairs too either/or has caused an immeasurable harm. Either you are my friend or else an enemy, either you are with Russia or with America, either you are a Hindustani or you are a Pakistani, either you are a communist or you are the blue-eyed boy of the capitalist, either you are an admirer of 'X' in literature and 'Y' in music or an enemy, etc. In the opinion of many, this system of Aristotelian logic is inherent in the very nature of intelligence; it is an eternal truth. It is a matter of great relief that scholars of modern Greek civilization have clearly shown that Aristotelian logic was a reflection of a declining Greek civilization and that prior to the decline, when Greek society was closely knit, a different system of logic was in use. Not only that, Korzybski, a Polish scholar and the President of the Non-Aristotelian Society, in his path-breaking book *Science and Sanity*, has proved that in all the branches of European knowledge—he had examined almost twenty—this syllogistic Aristotelian system of logic has so confused man's intellect that the whole world has today become a lunatic asylum. Personalism does not have this 'versus-sense'. Instead, there is an 'integral-sense', the logic of which is primarily dialectic, similar to the rules of 'composition' and 'association' of John Stuart Mill which he deemed fit for the study of society. Thus the freedom of personalism (*purushavada*) is not a 'static concept', it is 'dynamic'. The two kinds of freedom—the freedom to oppose others and the freedom gained through cooperation which in turn enables one to perform higher deeds—are entirely different from each other. The similarity is only in the physical form of the individual and person.

A cooperative person is real, an individual is not. This is precisely the meaning of the idea that man is a social animal. Man is born, leads his life and dies within the ties of society. The circles of society are various: in the first circle or the 'primary group', life is closely linked to biology and is based on physical ties. In the next circle, which is the secondary group, man seeks to free himself from the animal world. We could have traced back the roots of individual freedom to this secondary group had freedom been the only object behind the formation of this group. Fortunately even in forming secondary groups the task of group building is primary and in the process new ties and new regulations become necessary. Thus it continues and in the process man forms various types of groups; each is more open than the other, yet not outside the purview of rules and regulations. *Swaraj* means abiding by self-imposed rules. During childhood the rules set by mothers and grandmothers seem to be as ineluctable as destiny; in adult life, membership of science societies seems to be as good as a free choice. Man's gradual advancement from being under the domination of nature to his observance of polite behaviour of civilized society is nothing but the historical evidence of his gradual emancipation, and his indomitable desire to move from one boundary to another. In this lies the limit to determinism and individual freedom. The 'person' does not lose his way within the two limits, but the 'individual' is likely to be confused. Those familiar with the essence of such poems of Rabindranath as *'shimar majhe ashim tumi'* ('within bounds, yet You are infinite') will find it easy to comprehend the meaning of the term 'person'.

This concept of personalism—the proposition of the new philosophy— has to be distinguished from the proximate idea of another kind of personalism. The belief in an indestructible soul recognizes the existence of a 'personality' even after death. Such a realization may be natural after a relative passes away. However, in the present context, I am not referring to that but to the concept of 'personality' in Christianity. The idea of building a model of personality after Christ, or of attaining God's favour through him is defunct. In another essay I have mentioned Lord Shaftesbury. He was a Tory, a devout man and the maker of English laws in favour of the Christian working class. Those who have read his autobiography know that his will to reform was driven neither by hatred for the wealthy nor by love for the workers, but by the ideal of Jesus Christ. And because of this ideal he was against any labour movement. Thus, Christianity's 'grace' heals the wounds of the exploited but fails to dislodge the exploiter. Today many Catholics have become almost socialists. A lot of people have heard about the Red Deans. In France they have displayed their true colour. If the expulsion of man from heaven is the beginning of human history and if attaining heaven is its end then man-made history is nothing more than the Parsi theatre's comic interludes between two acts of the *Mahabharata* play. If there is nothing else in man's work and effort there is at least dignity. An individual does not have any sense of dignity. Several Christian scholars however have found a tragic dignity in Christian personalism. But the judgment and character of the Christian community that is lording over the world today only remind us of a drunken jester. The harm that its particular brand of individualism will cause to the rest of the world unawares will be the real tragedy. There is no relation whatsoever between this and the Christian 'tragic sense of being in Christ on the cross'.

Another type of personalism has to be avoided. Primitive societies used to 'personalize' both enemies and friends. The type of developed cognitive ability required to think of power as an impersonal force was either not available to them, or else their mode of reasoning was different. Whichever the case might be, transforming an external force to an embodied person is a common feature of primitive societies. This feature is concretized through the patterns of rituals, customs and manners. Consequently, social stratification begins. From the beginning, society has been divided into two classes: that of leaders, priests, bards and others of upper social classes who are adept at conceiving of power as personified and making other people do the same; and that of the lower classes—who are the rest and incapable of facing the forces of nature. However grateful we might be to anthropomorphism (i.e., ascribing a human form to God) for providing the foundation of social customs, we have to remember that it is also responsible for perpetuating the two classes and thus for maintaining social ties. From leader to leadership, from shaman to priesthood, from minstrel to court-poet—when such various functions emerged, the power internal to every function, viz., the power to intimidate people or to deliver them from fear and thereby carrying on with the work and claiming it to be the best and the only and eternal truth was only covered up by human relations and not transformed. What this fear is will become evident if I refer to anthropomorphism. Rabindranath provides the best example of this in his book *Personality*. He says that we have domesticated our gods and have made them our relatives: Durga is our daughter; she comes to her parental home and goes back to her in-laws' place and this is celebrated in the songs of *agomoni* and *bijoya*. Instead of asking whether this 'we' refers to the Bengalis, the Indians or each of the ancient races, I may provide another example of the same process of 'humanization'. There is *Ma Shitala* for pox, *Ola Debi* for cholera etc. When we make *Shitala* a mother and *Ola* a *Debi* just the way we address any Bengali lady we surely humanize them; and the virulence of pox and cholera are still such that such an institution as the Calcutta Corporation has not been able to bring them under control. Today if an Oriya brahmin comes to the doorstep with an idol of *Shitala* or *Ola* then even a modern housewife is not unwilling to part with a few coins for this humanized power. She is apprehensive lest anything happens to her darling baby if she does not contribute. We indeed warmly welcome Durga but deep within us there is also the fear that all might not be well for the family if we do not do so. In Gandhi's lifetime many of his staunch followers were afraid of him lest they did something that went against his ideas as he stood for India's welfare and independence. Many disapproved of his ways, but did not dare to pursue any other. There were times when he would make a suggestion to the Congress committee which would draw forth serious opposition. In such cases, he would say, 'Do as you please and let me do as I please. Please leave me.' Many of his followers would compare such behaviour, his abstinence from food and frequent fasts, with holding a gun to their heads. Yet his words prevailed because it would have been unfair to defy him, after all he was *kalyana* personified. People both revered and feared this figure. If we are so apprehensive of even such a prophet of love then imagine what it must be like with others. We have followed his advice and almost won our independence; so our faith in him as *kalyana* personified must have helped. But we have to admit that because of this idol worship we did not get the time to think on our own. Otherwise even Jawaharlal would not have confessed that 'we have been taken unawares'—not once or twice, but several times. Similarly, Gandhian socialism, an absurdity, would not have sold in the market as gold; or the taunting and despising any of the leftist groups would not have been considered a sign of unadulterated patriotism. The being of anthropomorphism is not a part of humankind. It emerges from the common man's incomprehension of power. It is not a human being of flesh and blood; it is a phantom taking on a human form. This is indeed a part of human civilization; but, just as much as doctors consider an appendix to be a part of the human body—a dispensable part. However, it is not desirable that the social body should suffer from peritonitis.

It has already been stated that a person is born in a primary group and then he moves beyond it. There is no end to his spheres. It is unbearable for him to remain within a clan, or a tribe because even such ties consume his entire human essence. However, the existence of these social spheres is not affected by the survival of the person. For the person, the expansion of the spheres is necessary to enlarge the domains of his recognition, to enhance his income and to win battles. A person therefore seeks to create larger associations, companionships, collaborations and cooperatives against which he can evaluate his humanity. This constant desire to move on is the true mark of personalism; and this is different from both the 'heterenomous' personality of Hindu society and the asocial 'a-nomous' personality of Euro-American society; because this is 'autonomous'. And, this is precisely the reason why a person is equally eager to earn his rights and to judiciously and painstakingly discharge his responsibilities. It is in the person that rights and duties combine. It is possible for rights in one sphere to be transformed to responsibilities in another only when a person, integrated in society, facilitates a constantly progressing social circle instead of indulging in oppositions like individual versus society or state. To a progressive social being there is no unrealistic conflict between rights and responsibilities.

There is yet another contradiction that is resolved in personalism. The issues of opposition between tradition and experimentation are prevalent in literature, music, art and science. As long as man is asocial, unreal, an ordinary speck of humanity, there is meaning in this opposition. People believe that those who follow tradition are conservative and those who experiment are progressive. Not only that, they also believe you are either this or that; and, this and that are eternal enemies. This is the same 'either/or' logic. A person is born in the womb of tradition and on the strength of his works he comes out into life's testing grounds. The same human being bears the burden of tradition and moves forward, sometimes lessening the burden and sometimes taking up new burdens without any qualms. This kind of selective continuity, this gradual unfolding, is the only independence that the person enjoys. When European socialists consider Western democracy to connote individual independence, it is understandable to a certain extent because the concept of the individual emerges from European perception and experience. However for an Indian socialist to say that the difference between democratic socialism and other kinds of socialism lies in individual freedom is illogical. However disintegrated Indian society might have become, it has not yet turned to a garbage heap of discrete individual entities. In its mode of behaviour, conduct, and attitude to life it still reflects a concept of human nature that is more conducive to a theory of the person than that of the individual. It is not that Hindu society—we may also include the Muslim—did not get in the way of personalism; if that were the case then there would have been no reason for regret. However, while deciding the foundation of a new society if we have to choose between the deductive, fragmented, floating, rootless, and in that sense independent, individualism of European societies, and the integrated, concrete, and in that sense norm regulated, human beings of Indian civilization then we can assuredly go for the traditional way. We just have to be alert about whether the social responsibilities of our second and third social circles are impeding the rights of the next social circles. In our society the largest social circle is that of caste, beyond that is the circle of the spirit of the deceased—of course this is also a spectrum of the caste group. And ultimately, there is Brahma—beyond the mundane world. But we cannot call that a circle. In the interim circle there are groups of philosophers and *sanyasis* whose regular annual meeting at the *kumbha mela* is a miraculous event in the chapters of world history. But in the mean time, in India there has arisen another mid-level group like the economic class whose traces we might find if we search ancient history, but whose clear manifestations we have seen only in recent years. We cannot ignore them in creating a new social philosophy. However, we also cannot forget the first premise of a theory of personalism; class structures have to be kept open. Open class structure is the hallmark of a truly democratic society, and in such a society personhood may fully blossom. What the character of that open society will be only soothsayers can tell. To the extent that I have understood Marx and Engels it seems that they had something akin to this theory of personalism in mind.

4

Marxism and Humanism

The major charge against Marxism is that it does not assign any space to the individual. Many have replied to this charge. Of the rebuttals, two are bound to be accepted by all: (i) most people lose their individuality under the repressive social system of capitalism and therefore without the abolition of capitalism, there will not be any opportunity for the expression of individuality; and (ii) even the lucky few who have had an opportunity to develop their individuality in this society have not utilized it fully. Proof of this can be seen in the unfulfilled life of the workers and of the Babbitt class. Besides, people at other social levels are also so preoccupied with their struggle for existence, and so worn out by economic exploitation that individuality is nothing but a complete fiction to them, not to speak of its fulfilment. This is the common predicament of the teachers, artists, scientists and other intellectuals. Yet such a retort is negative in the ultimate analysis, for it does not logically follow that because man is shrinking in his stature under capitalism, he will have a fully developed individuality in a Marxist society. This is where you have the debate about Russia. Some say that man there is being crushed by a grindstone while others observe that all human beings have become supermen. Since I have not been to that country I shall accept only this that people there have regained their self-confidence. But the Americans, too, have self-confidence. There is certainly a difference between the two, but it is not suggested in the apologia for Marxism that has just been mentioned.

We need a different answer and need to look at it from a different angle. Human civilization has witnessed frequent conflicts between Nature and

DIPENDU CHAKRABORTY, Sir Gurudas Banerjee Professor, Department of English, University of Calcutta, has translated 'Marxism and Humanism' (originally titled 'Marxvada O Manushyadharma', written in 1947–48).

Community in terms of thought and behaviour. The so-called primitive tribes had a cosmology as well as an anthropology. Speculating on the origin of the visible and invisible worlds the primitive man also asked questions about his own origin. At first there was a supernatural explanation, then came mythology. Religion grew out of this, and instead of destroying the myths, religion nurtured them. As a result, what was just a natural impulse for knowledge gradually became an obligation to know what man is. With this change in thinking, man was alienated from the unbroken unity of nature, that is, the concept of totality. So far nature was an impersonal totality, man had no separate entity. But the urge for self-knowledge cut off man's bond with the external world, resulting in interrogation and scepticism. It is indeed surprising to see how this awareness of the self and sceptical attitude emerged in the initial stage of human civilization. That was, indeed, the beginning of what is called humanism. We see in the history of philosophy: 'Scepticism has very often been simply the counterpart of a resolute humanism. By the denial and destruction of the objective certainty of the external world the sceptic hopes to throw all the thoughts of man upon his own being' (Cassirer, *What is Man?*).

The Marxist theoretical discourse is related to this scepticism, though this gets suppressed by other Marxist tenets. The period of scepticism and self-awareness persisted for a long time. Hinduism, Buddhism, Judaism, Islam formed different chapters of this narrative. The gain from all this was that man could not forget that he was the centre of the universe. But there was considerable loss too, because the self was over-emphasized, the very existence of man was at stake. In other words, the totality called nature was reduced to a point called individual. The Copernican and Cartesian mode of thinking was a reaction against this. Man again felt his own vulnerability pitted against the whole universe. Man shrank in stature. Historians have not paid much attention to this aspect of the Renaissance, they are quite content quoting Hamlet's famous glorification of man. Montaigne wrote:

> Can anything be imagined so ridiculous, that this miserable and wretched creature; who is not so much as master of himself, but subject to the injuries of all things; should call himself master and emperor of the World, of which he has not the power to know the least part, much less to command the whole? (This was towards the end of the sixteenth century. At that time there was a new wave of humanism in India, thanks to the efforts of *sadhus* and saints. There was nothing like the Copernican and Cartesian system propagating a philosophy of nature in the realm of our thought and action. But this is not the place to assess its results.)

Now a question was raised—how could man free himself from the shackles of nature? If man is just a part of nature, in what ways are the laws of human affairs, that is, of society, history, state, culture, and conduct, different from the laws of nature? Mathematics, according to Copernicus and Descartes, determines human behaviour because the essence of Nature lies in numbers. This science of mathematical calculation brought man back to his earlier position. The concept of infinity proved that man could grasp the inherent mystery of universal nature with his rational faculty and observation, and that since nature is not confined to this earth, he can reach out to the firmament. Thus man again got back his faith in himself with the help of mathematics and other allied subjects. It was not a simple matter. Until the end of the nineteenth century attempts were made to reduce all human phenomena to mathematics—if you remember such names as Bucklaw[?], Fechner, Solvay, Edgeworth, etc.

But biology asserted itself against the generalization and deductive method of mathematics. Thanks to Darwin, the inductive method and empirical observation were used extensively. Chemistry had already developed fifty years ago. Man was not immediately dissociated from nature with the emergence of biology; rather he became more dependent on her, as is seen in the social theories of Comte, Herbert Spencer, Shuffle[?], etc. Taine wrote somewhere that he would write the history of France after the French Revolution as the 'metamorphosis of an insect'. Yet the result was quite opposite from two different angles: (i) According to biology a life-pattern was found which seemed to have helped man to outdo other animals in controlling nature with his own effort. And (ii) this history of progress is believed to have been directed towards an unforeseen goal. The philosophy of social progress, that has developed from the inception of the French Revolution till the present day, has behind it this teleology, faith in man, his present glory and his trust in the future. This teleological philosophy of social progress is the essence of what we call Humanism. Had man been confined to mathematics he could not have liberated himself fully from the laws of nature. (Cassirer could not appreciate the philosophy of progress, as Christopher Dawson very effectively demonstrated.) Once the path was discovered, all the studies concerning man moved forward, for example, psychology, history, economics, sociology, anthropology, not one was left behind.

But a new danger emerged. Every science has a dilemma: to advance means to fall into the pit of general laws of nature, not to advance would lead to the useless accumulation of facts described in detail. It is the same old debate: which one is more important: the general or the particular? If the general is accepted human history would either come under the purview

of mathematics or become 'natural history'. Again, if the particular is accepted, it will be impossible to build a general law, and nothing can be either
done or understood. Some historians have said that history must be written
like science, for example, Ranke. Some others like Carlyle have said that
history is a part of literature. Of course in their writings they never followed
their own views. Another problem was that every study of man made its
own rules and claimed that no other rules can be applied in the case of man.
Under the pressure of such conflicting claims the philosophical foundation
built in the sixteenth and seventeenth century collapsed. We still hear the
lament over this loss, as in Cassirer's *An Essay of Man* (pp. 21, 22).

But I think there is no cause for regret. Marxism compensates for this
loss. According to Marxism, man is part of Nature, yet he is independent,
that is, man can understand, criticize and mould as he pleases not only
human nature but also inanimate nature with his intelligence, judgment
and action. One finds here not the rigidity of the Copernican–Cartesian
methodology, but the dynamics of a whole process. Many people want to
categorize it as a kind of environmentalism; but if such an association has
to be made, it would be reasonable to link it with human geography. There
is no room for blind fate or sudden accident in Marxism. Just as man found
his freedom in the context of infinity, he can acquire faith in himself because
of his commitment to dialectical materialism. The methodology of Marxism
is primarily inductive, deductive in special cases. Its main tenet is the observation of the life-process, its examination, generalization, classification, and
comprehensive study, and from this inclusive definition and belief, grasping
the particularity of human activity. In Marxism the conflict between the
general and the particular has been resolved to a certain extent. Not only
that, Marxist history has been different from natural history because of
this. This view of progress is not the unknown teleological progress as envisaged by Godwin or Condorcet. Because it is founded upon human effort,
it is so sound, yet so uncertain despite its certainty. As a matter of fact,
Marxism is a modern version of the old Humanism. Needless to say, it is
different from self-centred stoic humanism; it is unlike the self-analysis of
Indian humanism; it is opposed to the erratic profiteering individualism
generated by the Renaissance humanism in its last phase. It is also quite different from today's scientific humanism.

Thus it becomes abundantly clear: man is at the centre of Marxism. But
is man and individual the same thing? If it is said that only the individual is
real, since it has a body and a mind, then everybody will agree that the
relationship of Marxism with the individual being is not direct but through
a human community. In other words, the individual can be free only when

that community is liberated. If anybody says that there is nothing called the 'individual', which is only an imaginary concept and that the collective is all that matters, because the individual is affected, directed and determined by the collective, then Marxism has a direct engagement with humanity as a whole. I personally believe and not without reason, that 'individual' is a huge abstraction, which originated in the age of capitalism in England and that it has nothing to do with Indian thought or with events or society in India. *Purusha* is of central importance in Indian philosophy. Not many individuals have been born in our society yet whose life history can encourage the acquiring of wealth and position. Of course some have already made their presence felt. The moot point of individualism is economic progress. *Purushavada* has at its core the theory of *varnasrama*, that is, the emergence of the silkworm cutting through its cocoon after its growth within a social habitat. I am not suggesting that Marxism and Hinduism are the same thing. What I am trying to say is that Indians are not in a position to judge Marxism in the light of individualism. Only the rich and the English knowing people in India can claim this privilege. But are they really Indians? Marxism may have other drawbacks, but one cannot criticize Marxism because it does not make a special provision for the enrichment of the imaginary entity called an individual or the so-called discourse on it. To do so is to go against the very movement of the total human endeavour and to show a lack of respect for the history of knowledge. Humanism is related to Marxism through *Purushatatva* (personalism), not through individualism.

5
Intellectuals and Society

S ome sort of independence has at last been achieved—so, what should be our duty now? The answer to this question has to be found quickly, and so simply and beguilingly communicated to the masses that they believe in it for their own self-interest, and accept it of their own free will. The self-interest, moreover, should not be taken to be restricted to the present time alone; if we cannot keep in mind distant horizons and take the future into consideration, the progress of the nation will be stifled. Here lies the challenge for the intellectuals. They alone find it possible to compromise their popularity, while this is impossible for the politicians. The vision of the savant is not befuddled by present circumstances, nor is his movement confined like a dog's, trapped within a chalk circle.

The first question to ask then, is—what is the nature of this independence? We need not spend time deliberating whether the British were righteous or not; those at the helm of our free nation have asserted that they departed in good faith, so even if there were ulterior motives, we need to believe, along with our leaders, that our independent nation can surmount their ill effects. Without this faith we demean ourselves and betray the promise of our independence. This is not to claim that we have nothing more to fear with the removal of British imperialism. There is still the need to be, and to remain, wary, but this should no longer be our primary concern. Many, though, still continue to prioritize these fears. It is difficult to say how far their thoughts are affected by the past, or to what extent they are scientific. In my opinion, we have understood the machinations underlying the retreat, and even the changing forms, of British colonialism, and I think we shall continue to do

KRISHNA SEN, Professor, Department of English, University of Calcutta, has translated 'Intellectuals and Society' (originally titled 'Atah kim' or What Now?', written in 1947–48).

so. There are times when self-confidence is tantamount to self-deception; at other times, the illusion of strength fortifies the mind. We say this not for the sake of argument, but from a deep conviction. Ridding ourselves of excessive scepticism can only be for our good. Not till then shall we be able to perceive the true lineaments of our independence.

As of now, however, 'independence' is a meaningless term. Even Jawaharlal [Nehru] has admitted that the administrative system has broken down. True, there is no starvation in the country as yet, but it is not enough to say that. The mind-set of the nation has changed rapidly; tempests are to be expected. But what has this turbulence done to the two parts of India? Hatred for the British has been supplanted by hatred between Hindus and Muslims, and we have to admit that this hatred has severely undermined our powers. If we weigh our independence in the balance, it does not appear that its positive aspects have displayed themselves this year. The Asian Conference has been held, our ambassadors have been posted to a few places, we can perhaps cobble together some such instances as these, but the column at the left of the balance sheet is practically empty. Indeed, we may say that the discreditable things are more noticeable. Feudalism is still there, and in many provinces the labourer continues to be exploited; and yet we claim to be independent. It is the lot of the unfortunate to pursue elusive pleasures; opportunity knocks at the door and goes away unheard. We have to see to it from now that this does not happen to us. The leaders of the Congress as well as the [Muslim] League have meditated long and hard on these matters—then why do we still act so mindlessly? A little contemplation will make it clear that, in order to realize the true spirit of independence, we need to follow some other approach. The main thrust should be, not to critique the opponent, but to analyse oneself. We must change our modes of thought.

The very first component of this change is to scrutinize our leadership. If ever in the history of India this was necessary, it is so now, at this very moment. The rebellion that could have erupted because of the partition of Bengal and Punjab would have been fuelled by emotion, not reflection. I am speaking of the need for analysis. Of course mistimed criticism is also pointless. It provokes rancour without achieving anything positive. The Communist Party became less effective partly because of this reason. The Socialist Party is analytical enough, but its failure to fully realize its potentialities is due to other factors; it is frittering away its energies in opposing both the Congress and the Communist Parties in order to maintain its separate identity. In an era in which the re-orientation of ideas ought to be the responsibility of the Party, and not of individuals, a common programme for all the Left parties should have been the most feasible option. Unfortunately, there seems little likelihood of this. It will only materialize when workers and peasants exert pressure from below. Therefore in my opinion, every Left party must move closer to the workers and peasants and make common cause with them in order to make our independence meaningful. Needless to say, this will be a source of friction with the Congress Party. But what else is there to do?

I shall give an example of change in other kinds of thinking when these connections are firmly established. 'Other kinds of thinking' does not necessarily mean fruitless speculation. There is currently a lot of theorizing about assets and liabilities. Specialists have been called in, and we are being told that there is nothing as complicated as this. Of course we must admit that the matter is complex. But we must also pinpoint why it is so. The common man has no relevant facts at his disposal, whatever little information there is, is lodged with the government, and even then it is in disorder since our government has instituted no serious inquiry into this matter. No one knows what the national income is. The British have no faith in such information. It is only during the last few years that budgets along with accounts relating to the national income have been placed before the Parliament. To my mind, our leaders have inherited their contempt for facts from the British. The second reason for our lack of information is that it would be disastrous to reveal the real truth about division of assets, and therefore the main point is deliberately shrouded in confusion. The main point is that division of assets is not division but multiplication, for it is capital accumulation. Only those who have thought about the process of capital accumulation know that there are many states and strata in it according to which the amount and movement of the financial assets are determined. The Indian trader is becoming wealthy. India's problem is to find ways of converting trade and commerce into instruments of wealth production. There are at least two ways of doing this— (1) use the surplus capital after expenses to acquire assets, and (2) a few capitalists can either jointly, or with help from banks, acquire the titles of ownership of these assets. This stage relates to the primary issue of *acquisition*. The next stage relates to *realization*, that is, transforming the ownership of the means of production into an instrument of the productive process. Currently both methods of acquisition are being followed in our country, though there is a historical bias towards the second mode. However, when saved capital is insufficient for the process of realization, one needs to turn to finance groups or bank capital. Hence division of assets is bound to work towards concentration of ownership of titles, or in other words, monopolies. Moreover, there is bound to be a time lag between acquisition and realization because of the shortage of capital goods. The more the titles of ownership change hands during this period, the more profitable it is [for the capitalists]. Everybody knows the condition of the share market. The owner always wishes to sell at a higher price and buy at a lower. A powerful owners' and buyers' lobby can compel the government to adjust the value of goods and titles in its favour. This is what happens in every country, and it is happening, and will happen in this country as well. We also know that even without the connivance of the government the united efforts of the capitalist class can influence the market for its own ends. So much for the real nature of the division of assets, which is merely another name for capital accumulation. It is undeniable that capital accumulation is required for the progress of the nation. But whose responsibility is it to accumulate this capital, and to what end? If we assume that this obligation is the government's, and that its end or function is the improvement of the lifestyle of the people, then the whole affair of the division of assets becomes very simple. For this eliminates the rotation of ownership of assets; market value is no longer geared to private profit in the interlude between acquisition and realization, but is so determined as to serve the interests of the masses. Our economists and intellectuals have only to bear the lives of the common people in mind to avoid their current perplexity. This explains my insistence that we must revolutionize our thinking. And for that we must set up solid contacts with people. Else we will be cheated by the vicious calculations of the market. Mr Ghanashyamdas Birla's assets have been seen as a 'fetish'. Economists too have not told us to view them differently, and this is causing bewilderment. But the point at issue is—for whose sake is this division of assets, for whose benefit is this independence? My reason for being so emphatic is that, within the next few months, and taking advantage of this magnificent confusion, the rich will get richer. It is time for our economists to think independently. They bear an enormous responsibility under these circumstances. But if they fail to identify with the new social class, they run the risk of being arrogant rather than responsible. What we urgently require today, then, is sound economic leadership, and the power base for economic leadership is contact with the masses. We must never overlook this fact.

Another element of radical change in our thinking must be the establishment of a new relationship with the Muslim community. Even though I reside at a place where Hindu–Muslim antipathy has not yet polluted personal connections, I am well aware of the extent of hostility. Only the other day, in Sitapur district, the August revolutionary and socialist Mohanlal Gautam was defeated at the polls by a Hindu Sabha candidate, the son of a *talukdar*. The entire local Congress unit was supporting Gautam. Such an eventuality was unheard of in this region. It is clear that [communal] antagonism has spread far and wide. Nevertheless, it must be eradicated. Bengal has been

partitioned and that is cause enough for regret. At one time we had opposed
Partition, but this time we actually asked for it. The saddest thing is that we
have not really understood why we agitated for the re-uniting of the sundered
parts then. The superficial motive was nationalism, but the underlying
purpose was the instinctive desire to perpetuate the [feudal benefits of the]
Permanent Settlement. This time, too, we shall ask for re-unification, but
not for the sake of the Permanent Settlement. Re-unification is only possible
if we discard that institution completely. It will begin to break down the
very day the state of Pakistan comes into being. If we have truly changed
our point of view, we should assist Pakistan in its dissolution. I do not say
that this alone will alleviate our mutual mistrust; but a combined effort to
eliminate feudalism may just open up the possibility of creating something
new, and the creative collaboration may bring about the union of hearts. So
far the ongoing endeavours were inspired neither by sincerity nor sense, but
only by ineffectual idealism—hence, so incongruous a project as 'Muslim
mass contact', which was not only unsuccessful but produced the opposite
of what was intended. This is a Marxist interpretation. The masses were not
afforded the opportunity to do anything creative; and of the common people,
it is the Muslims who constitute the largest segment of the labouring and
peasant classes who are exploited, subjugated, and unlettered. We need to
be absolutely clear about this simple fact; if our vision is blinkered by idealism,
we shall be incapable of appreciating the true nature of an independent
India. There is no other explanation for our so-called solicitude for the
Muslims. However, the campaign for a united Bengal is unconnected with
this issue.

Yet another instance: our leaders have exhibited a similar attitude towards
the native princely states, regardless of what they have actually said. This is
not a special case. We have seen it even in colonial times—the many disasters
brought about in this world by the notion of 'trusteeship'. That idea has
been resurrected again in this country. The Mahatma has called upon the
princes as well as the capitalists to act as the trustees or guardians of the
underprivileged; even Jawaharlal is advocating a variant of constitutional
monarchy. But this was not fully successful even in the nineteenth century,
and today it is absolutely irrelevant. We now have to ask for a people's
government. We must also take good care that the common people do not
become puppets in the hands of the capitalists. 'Balkanisation' may well
spread beyond the Balkan Peninsula. The native states appear to crystallize
all the problems of contemporary India. They are hotbeds of feudal and
foreign capitalist conspiracy. Only the new Indian class has the capacity to
withstand them; neither the Congress nor the League has the power. Very

fortunately, this is not a major issue in Bengal; the Bengali can in fact take some satisfaction in comparing the present condition of Bengal with that of the highly taxed native states.

I have referred only to a few problems and their solutions in this article. When viewed together, they raise but a single issue—how are we to change our existing attitudes? As an intellectual I have but one suggestion: to peruse the causes and the consequences of all the major civil wars in the history of the world. We have for some years now been reading the socialist classics, and this has on the whole been of benefit to us. Now we also need to read accounts of internecine conflicts, especially that of America (as for example, Leo Huberman's *We the People*). We must know about the internal schisms in Spain and China. However, studiousness by itself is not likely to further the nation's cause. We must be attached to one political party or another. Which party? We are alive to the deficiencies of each of the Leftist parties in the country. Their main drawback is the bickering amongst themselves. This has had catastrophic effects in Germany and destroyed Austria—we know it all. Hitler's rise to power was facilitated by the enmity between the Social Democrats and the Communist Party. The writings of the Austrian socialist leaders such as Otto Bauer and Brunthal clearly demonstrate how they were paralysed at the time of crisis despite their intelligence and sincerity. And yet, even that country has not learnt the lesson of history, so what hope can there be for us? Over here, 'social democracy' and 'communism' are no more than trite slogans. Hence books cannot unify the Left parties. This is where we need to be analytical. Should we say that the controversies within the Left are the consequences of personal rivalry?

It is my good fortune to be acquainted with the leaders of several parties. Are any of them deficient in their understanding of history? Not at all. Some of them, indeed, are intellectuals of a high calibre. Do some of them have less sensibility than others? That, too, does not appear to be the case. Do some of them love their country more than others? I do not possess the means to measure love, but all of them have served prison sentences [in the cause of the nation], all of them have made heroic sacrifices. And every single party rests its hopes on the labourer and the peasant.

Their different ideologies are also not the problem. My experience has taught me that a person is effective in proportion to his connection with new forces. There are no different opinions about what the new forces are. The difference lies in establishing the connection. The internal wrangling among the Left parties is due to none of them being seriously engaged with the worker and the peasant. I do not mean to criticize but only to analyse why the Left has failed to unite. To some extent this is due to lack of maturity among the workers and peasants as well. But are they really so immature? My opinion is—they are not. If this belief is correct, then the Left will soon come together. Failing this, there is no satisfactory answer to the question— 'What now?' But if my thinking is incorrect, then there remains the responsibility to increase awareness. And that responsibility rests squarely with the intellectuals, and with no one else.

PART TWO

REFLECTIONS ON HISTORY

6
The Meaning and Method of History

In the civilized world there is always a specific need to develop a concept of history. It is in relation to this attitude that the sequence of events or their characteristics are revealed. Otherwise, man will drift along in the current of circumstances like a straw, life will lose its meaning and worth. Even a person who is not consciously eager to seek meaning in life, even he whose chief concern or habit is to somehow earn a livelihood, is pained by the worthlessness and meaninglessness of life. A little analysis will show that a vague concept of history works behind the pittance of worth that even a mere routine existence has. Those who are not in conflict with the outer and the inner world, that is, those who are opposed to any kind of change, feel that after their demise the world will go to the dogs, the pace of history will slow down. The views about history of those who want to return to an imaginary world or try to establish paradise on this earth is a mere poetic version of the above attitude. Revolutionaries think that the pace of history is quickening and moving towards a Utopia. Its pace is like that of a frog, not of a turtle. To them the pace of history consists in a movement towards improvement. So to survive happily in this society, to get respite from this society, or to construct a new society after destroying the old one, one must realize this goal of history because on this depends how to have a better and even better quality of life by achieving an adjustment with one's surroundings.

Just for the sake of argument one may assume that the non-societal man need not have any concept of history. Actually there is no such individual who is a non-societal man. Robinson Crusoe belonged to a society before being marooned on an island and the culture he had derived from that

ANASUYA GUHA, Reader, Department of English, Lady Brabourne College, Calcutta, has translated 'The Meaning and Method of History' (originally titled 'Itihasa 1' or 'History 1', written in 1933–34).

society determined the way he acquired food on the island, or the way he behaved with the savages. His eagerness to return to that society was not abated either. In other words, the condition of Crusoe reminds one of those who reject society today to live in *ashrams*. The true sage performs penance to go beyond the temporal framework. But it does not seem that even he is free from history or from the need to develop an outlook towards history. The yogi or sage is engaged in thoughts of welfare of the entire universe. But unless one feels that the universe has suffered calamity and is moving towards a greater calamity there is no need for thoughts of welfare. Besides yoga has its history, the sage too has his history, the way society perceives the sage also has its own history.

The case of the intellectuals is no different. A basic question that lurks behind all attempts of philosophers is whether time and matter are a creation of the mind, or have a separate existence. Is change occasioned by endless time or is time an attribute of change? The basic concern of economics is ascertaining the price, even there the price level is determined over time. In the case of science too time has a role to play. Though 'history' is forbidden to enter the laboratory of the scientist, the history of experiments enters it by some loop-hole like the goddess Monosha. Einstein had tried to enslave time by means of mathematics. But if Michelson, Morley, Minkowski and Maxwell had not come before him, he might have become something else and not what he did become. In a nutshell, all knowledge is closely related to life, life is societal, so knowledge is one of the primary ways of establishing contact with society. Again when the establishment of a link or connection becomes impossible then the old society is destroyed with the help of science, and efforts are made to construct a new one. So every intellectual and every intelligent person has the duty of constructing the right attitude towards history. Anybody who is indifferent about this cannot bring about advancement in knowledge.

This is particularly true of today's India. The ruling class (belonging to a foreign race) has said: 'History proceeds slowly; it is so in England, our country, Edmund Burke's comment being proof of it; so first partial autonomy in provincial administration; after proving oneself, complete autonomy; then diarchy at Delhi; after proving oneself there, attainment of full independence as in Canada or Australia. The trend of Indian history ought to be so and therefore it will be so'. A certain group at least among the ruled are replying: 'We are ready, but in the meantime if we must place a few mutually acceptable conditions, then they must be implemented for our welfare and after some time they must be withdrawn'. Both groups agree that history means a gradual improvement—from Ho[?] to the supremely knowledgeable.

About twelve years ago we had slightly different ideas about history—if we had faith in the words of the Mahatma and had carried out his orders, we would have been opening the page of the *swaraj* chapter of history on a specified date. That idea no longer holds. This is the age of progress. This new idea is working also in the case of social reform. The caste Hindus (meaning Gandhiji and Malviyaji) are ready to allow the untouchables to enter the temples—but without tampering with the caste system. This may be termed the 'tortoise-reform' (*kamathasanskara*) of history.

Though the tortoise incarnation was conceived in this very country and the tortoise-like behaviour is an accepted mode of life, the aforesaid concept of history is not ours. Since no other concept has emerged from our work we have accepted a concept useful and conducive to the interest of the ruling class. As our scholars could evolve no definite theory about the aims and essence of history, we are blindly applying a borrowed theory in our country just as in nineteenth century England the theory of evolution in biology was used to explain the phenomenon of social evolution. This is emulation, not creation. So the difference is merely in rhythm, the ruling classes and Brahmins want a single rhythm, the ruled and the Harijans want it to be doubled. The tempo is the same. The gradual evolution and expression of the biological world are not applicable to human society, not even in England, especially now. Wrong imitation only wastes strength, it does not conserve it. India's responsibility is more than that of other countries for we have a great deal to do. Wastage is not only a sin, it is foolish.

Many may feel that there is no need to create a new concept of history in our country. They feel that the rotation of Satya, Treta, Dwapar or Kali millennia or the 'Plan of the Moment' (*Muhurta Parikalpana*) of Brahma will determine the interpretation and duty of this millennium.

In order to save this theory from the charge of non-feasibility the opinions of the civilized world, and especially that of German philosophers are cited. The lowest common multiple of Hindu *Purana* as well as of Nietzsche, Spengler etc. is this concept of cyclical change of the historical process. For the sake of truth it is enough to remember that the goal of the preaching of the Hindu *Purana* was spiritual (*Adhyatmik*), that of today's scholars is material (*Adhibhautik*), at the most supernatural (*Adhidaivik*), but the result is the same. Therefore it is possible to discuss these two concepts together. Compared to the large periphery of these cycles, the cycle of our familiar civilized era is so small that every effort of man becomes fruitless. The search for meaning that necessitates an interpretation of the nature of history should not begin with a reminder of futility or a loss of self-confidence. If man is excluded, history loses meaning, at least to man. The gist of the matter is that in the ancient past when man had not been able to make the external relationships meaningful, it was not possible for him to discover any law or norm about either the sequence or the extent of time. Very recently we have become aware of our past, and with its help we have begun to understand the motion and laws of the passage of time and to interpret the existence of the present and the progress of the future. So far our idea has not become fixed and firm, it has not become transformed into a steady contemplation. This rather nebulous idea, being excluded from the consideration of the scientist, hides its face in shame. But the change that is seen as being born from the Yoga slumber of Brahma only to be surely merged into it again, the movement, the knowledge of whose secret purpose is a mere birthright of an individual or a class with certain virtues, such change is not true change, but a dream of it. Such a view may give ample scope for wish fulfilment but it cannot explain the stark and brutal reality of the present day world. It does not express the innermost secrets of diversity because the chanting of the 'And that too' (*Eva cha*) hymn can only achieve unity. What was; would remain; there would be no change in either appearance or spirit—such words befit only the Zarathustra of Nietzsche's imagination. An equation brought about by destiny is not different from one brought about by factories and machines. If one has to depend on Brahma or on His Will then the historian and the Brahmin become identical. This spells imminent danger for the non-Brahmins whose number is on the increase. Since in this Fallen Millennium (Kali Yuga) there are no Brahmins of the Puranic kind, the job of the historian also gets reduced. If the responsibility for discovering the nature of history is entrusted to the supernatural, then the Prussian state becomes the sole manifestation of Brahma, the Brahmin professor becomes one who has knowledge of Brahma and philosophy becomes a kind of egotistic creed—*Sohamvada*—the merging of the self with the Absolute Idea.

The aforesaid comment does not mean that we never had any history. The contention is that we are only now aware that we did have a history. In this sense all history is contemporary history. The meaning of history cannot be revealed with the help of the supernatural. The meaning is inherent in 'nature', though so much of the unnatural takes place in the action and behaviour of that 'nature' that it is totally inexplicable and so it is termed 'supernatural'. Only if seen thus can history be freed of the allegation of being a figment of the imagination. How our rituals have developed in contact with physical reality, how far we are subservient to fate, how much we ourselves have actively elected to do and how far we have been elected— knowledge of all this makes history something tangible. Else history becomes the literary creation of the imagination. In fact, the nearest kin to history is geography. There is no such thing as scientific history—events can be neither scientific nor unscientific, only their interpretation can be scientific. That is why the event to be interpreted, that is, the relation and sequence of events should be externalized as far as possible.

Man has formed society for survival. And his chief instrument is science. Today efforts are under way to consider science as a disinterested pursuit, but one cannot afford to forget that it took its origin in the needs of man. One of man's major problems was how to collect food from nature for survival. Science has come into being ever since the problem of food came into being. The economic factor has always been at the root of science, and that, factor is, to use a mathematical term, primary. In other words, no other theory can be used to explain this. Say an intelligent man of pre-historic times made an invention by which that race found it easier to collect food or to survive the depredations of enemies, to conserve a little strength, so that the race became powerful in a different sphere. Every invention of the pre-historic age had, as its cause and outcome, this will to survive, otherwise discoveries would not have been popular; in the competition between one discovery and another neither would have survived. When a discovery made a social group lead a better life than their former one, and a better life than those of others, then that society began to be constructed anew with the help of, and revolving round, that discovery. This is because society and science have an identical aim to enable us to survive and to lead a better life. The society which fails to produce an inventor or fails to emulate, is left behind in this struggle for survival. This went on for some time, that is, more and more novel inventions and newer ways of constructing society.

Moreover, the pace of discoveries is found to be greater than that of social reconstruction. Discoveries are made by a few people, but society comprises a large number of people. Those few can devote their entire leisure period to the task of creation. It is due to the variance in the pace of these two motions that social progress is possible. When hunting was the only way of acquiring food, then the mores of the hunter-society, relationships between man and man and between man and woman, property rules and religion were formulated around the profession of hunting. In the age of animal rearing it was found possible to acquire food cheaply with the help of animals. With the know-how regarding the taming of animals, new methods of farming became possible. Earlier, there were only combing the soil, *jhoom* plantation and gardening. The population started increasing, villages were formed, people started living in proper houses. It was necessary to provide them with a steady supply of food. It was then that the male became the patriarch, property assumed its present form, the heavens changed their form and God appeared on the stage in the guise of the male! Every age retained vestiges of the former one, no society was absolutely pure. Even the race which has embraced the industrial culture of factories and mills has not wholly rejected agriculture. Among the agricultural societies a specific class became rich by owning land and real estate. Small farmers failed to get two square meals a day, yet they were increasing in number. Another class became richer through commercial and mercantile activities. In the meantime the importance of older implements diminished. With the help of science and under the pressure of social need new implements were made. Money began to flow into the new factories from the two aforementioned classes. The excess population of the former society no longer remained redundant, many took jobs in factories, some went abroad. This has been happening only in a few countries in the last hundred and fifty years, and others are emulating them. In no other way can there be enough food supply for a large population.

But the wealthy class were the first to enjoy the fruits of the blessings of science. The ways of the historical process cannot be understood if one merely says that they are still enjoying those fruits. One must probe deeper. The first advancement brought about by science was in the mechanical sphere. As a result of this mills and factories multiplied. But though a machine feeds a large number of people, it also works in lieu of a large number of people. So the redundant population had to be driven away. But not too far. At first many migrated to other countries but later it was seen that it was to the mill owner's advantage that the workers stayed close by. The advantages were twofold—firstly, if demand increased then more people would be needed for the increased supply; secondly, if one group wanted a pay hike they would desist for fear of their jobs going to the other group of workers. In fact, at that time demand was indeed on the increase. It had taken on a different shape. It was necessary to have new factories for making new machines. England took up the task of making new machines. Some workers got jobs. Their wages were increased and their number too kept on increasing. In fact, their wages were not proportional to the increase in number. But science, that is, the means of producing for society by conquest of physical nature, does not let grass grow under its feet. It only knows that it has to give. Like a silly boy it does not know when to give, what to give, whom to give, how to give. At the outset it knew all this. But science has now become the profession of a class of people, a class whose creator is the rich, a profession which is parasitic, whose purpose is to discover ways and means of fulfilling the purposes of another class. Now the rich donated huge sums for scientific education, new types of universities were set up, massive laboratories were constructed, and scientists were employed at high pay in their own factories. But even if you can buy over scientists, you cannot buy over science. Here was a further danger. Just as a mill cannot stop, science too cannot stop. So the mill-owners started singing a different tune. They are saying today, 'To stop the progress of science for some time will be conducive to the welfare of the world'. They are buying patents and preserving them in iron chests. If production is increased haphazardly it leads to a reduction of profit which then has to be split up. So either science must come to an end or, with the help of science, loss must be reduced and profit increased. The latter is called scientific management or rationalization. But the purpose is the same—to ensure a high rate of profit. The means too is the same—to ensure a status quo so that workers continue to remain in their class. Today the scenario of our society is so miserable due to those scientists who are, or rather that 'science' which is, the slave of the rich.

The rich mill-owner class was not easily going to let go its power and influence. They were forced to adopt other means in order to get respite from science. Realizing the dangers of unlimited and open competition they decided to limit the area of competition. That is why for the past few years trusts, cartels and so on are becoming widespread in trade and commerce. Apart from a few co-operatives which had spread beyond the nation and the empire, all the rest are scattered over the country. But there was a depression in the market. So it was necessary to create a small zone. The dangers of competing with monopolies of other countries were also substantial. That is why these enormous co-operatives concentrated on spreading trade and commerce in the colonies. By the treaty of Versailles the rest of the world was parcelled out among the rich nations and the richer classes. Business in the colonies was much more lucrative, the market was larger, raw materials and labour cheap, and the ruling power was ready to help the merchants. If capitalism did not enter the colonies it would die due to sheer lack of space. The most advanced state of capitalism is monopoly and the colony provides the market for that. India has become embroiled in this syndrome of colonialism. Particularly so in the last few years, because Australia, Canada, South Africa, New Zealand are today nearly independent states, that is, the wealthy class is on the rise in those countries and wanting to increase their profit. The present condition of India can only be understood in the context of those historical forces which are the strongest in the world.

A mere statement of this will not suffice. Ostensibly the time is that of the predominance of capitalism. At least for Wells and his students, the world is becoming one. In various parts of the world alliances are being formed, it is natural to regard these as welcome symptoms of the establishment of a global empire. The British empire on the one hand, north and south America on the other. Three or four countries of the Balkan too have formed friendly alliances, there is a French–Pole–Czech alliance too. Apart from this the whole of Africa and Asia is part of some European empire or other. Still, somewhere, the evil eye is at work. In a certain part of the world only two years ago, in 1931, lakhs of *maunds* of wheat were burnt, coffee was ground and used in engines, extraction of petrol from mines and of rubber from rubber trees was prohibited at gunpoint. Cotton trees were razed to the ground with their trees and blossoms; those who produce sugar reduced production by devising a Five-Year Plan; in the mines the number of labourers and their working hours were reduced because copper, tin, lead and aluminium were being produced in large quantities. Because of factory-made liquor, the liquor trade of Chile was destroyed. But on the other hand, in other parts of the world people are starving, wages have been reduced, people cannot make two ends meet, more than twenty million labourers are unemployed, every nation is ready to export and unwilling to import. There are taxes on everything, major factories have closed down, the money market is moribund. The whole of Europe is indebted to America, but America will not take the repayment of the loan either in kind or by borrowing money. Germany has very little money, France has a lot of gold—there is havoc the world over, yet there is no end to gold the world over. What else can this be but the evil eye? The child nurtured by science and capitalism destroys science and capitalism when he grows up. This is the course that history takes.

In this essay the mainstream of history and only one of its courses has been mentioned. That stream is nourished by the accumulation of wealth and the history of science. The course that it takes shows that the seeds of destruction of any institution are inherent in that institution. The cause of the destruction is not God's will. The cause is that in a capitalistic system the rich desire the maintenance of the status quo, and by the grace of science there is always a plethora of new means of production. The stasis, progress and regression of this society should be explained scientifically—that is with the help of the history of man's combined need and effort to conquer outer nature or his attempts to do so. The history of India is a part of the history of the world, its distinguishing feature is its environment.

7

The Meaning and Method of History: European Experiences

The meaning and method of history has been suggested in the introduction.[1] The aim of this section of the essay is to illuminate this with illustrations.

Even though the mainstream of history is the same, it takes different forms and moves at a different pace due to the circumstances in different countries. In a country that has remained largely agricultural, where there has been neither discovery nor emulation of any other means of livelihood, the social structure depends fundamentally upon land ownership rights. In an agricultural country the relationship of the ryot and the feudal landlord becomes the basis of all social relationships. A thoughtful author by the name of Hopkins has written a book analysing the father–son relationship. In the third chapter of this book he has demonstrated how the son has always objected to the father's sole ownership of property and that this opposition has led to many revolutions in social codes. In his words, the position of the father in an agricultural society is that of a monopolist capitalist in modern society, that is, a capitalist who enjoys continuous ownership rights. Considering the paternal rights that prevailed at the inception of Roman Law and its gradual dwindling, one has to agree with Hopkins. We respect the Chinese civilization for being completely pious, steadfast and stable, and this is because it is clan based. Granay[?] has shown that among the Chinese the basis of the ideal father and son relationship is that of the

SANJUKTA DAS, Reader, Department of English, Presidency College, Calcutta, and Guest Lecturer, Department of English, University of Calcutta, has translated 'The Meaning and Method of History: European Experiences' (originally titled 'Itihasa 2' or 'History 2', written in 1933–34).

[1] That is, in the preceding chapter.

ryot's devotion to the feudal lord. In Egypt, too, this relationship based on land ownership right evolved into *mansabdari* and influenced other spheres of action and thought in society. India may have a history but it has no historian; therefore we do not know how knowledge about property in this agriculture-based country contributed to its social formations. One thing may however be stressed and that is, unless one knows the history of land rights in the Muslim and British periods, one cannot comprehend the history of folk society. On analysing our social customs, it is apparent how the subject–feudal landlord relationship is thoroughly entwined in social codes, in our marriage and other rituals, in the teacher–student relationship, in last rites, and in the mind-set of rural societies. The practice of calling God the King and the devotees His subjects is not new. Even the social set-up of Heaven depicted in the *Puranas* represents this society. Besides we also find this relationship to be particularly effective in the rise, expansion and decline of the Muslim empire. Domination by Muslim kings did not affect the historical tradition of India because they did not really interfere in the use and occupancy of land. Land use rights are being altered under the laws of the British period, therefore the pattern of our history too is changing. On one side there is the Permanent Settlement and on the other side there is the law relating to the rights of tenant farmers (*ryotwari*) and, partly as a result of this, the establishment of factories—which are the signposts of India in the present age.

That there are better means of livelihood than agriculture, we first came to know from the British. This is why I am discussing briefly the history of England. The change in the forms of livelihood in England from the late eighteenth century appeared so amazing to the people that it is regarded as a revolution. But another revolution had taken place quietly and unobserved even before and during this Industrial Revolution. Sheep rearing is needed for the wool business, therefore a lot of land is required together; therefore the fragments of land occupied by the cultivators were brought under the ownership of the landlord–businessman class. The parliament did not raise any objection as all members of the parliament were then from this class. The condition of villages in England were like those of other countries where the village and agriculture were dominant. One does not realize this by looking at the condition of England today, for England is the only country where, because of the change in means of production, that is, because of mills and factories, the history of social change has completed an entire phase. Until the end of the eighteenth century England was agriculture-based, (large-scale food grain was first imported only in 1792), much land was even then in the hands of small farmers. Many people were earning their livelihood from cottage industries. But at this time money from trade began to accumulate in the hands of the landlords. They used this money to buy new land, new machinery for agriculture; they brought down the price of grain by increasing yield through scientific methods of farming. Small farmers disappeared, cottage industry was destroyed, and land fragments came under the control of big landlords. One did not even have to take recourse to the law in order to occupy land; the consent of two thirds of the cultivators was enough. They had to consent. Consequently, from 1800 to 1819, 30 lakh acres of land came into the hands of landlords; in 1850 nothing remained. The farmers and villagers had lost their right to even the common land. It is not as though an Enclosures' committee did not sit down to lessen the travails of the poor; the farmers even received some money as compensation, but that money soon vanished. Sometimes cultivators evicted from the land and villages were compelled to go to the cities and join the mills and factories, else they went outside this landlord and tenant framework, to the new land of America.

Meanwhile the new owners of the mills and factories expressed a desire to become landlords. That is why during the war against Napoleon, the price of land was forty times the revenue. The old landlord community dwindled and marriages with the new rich began to take place. In 1830/40 at the time of the Reform Bill, in the whole of Europe it was in England that the largest average area of land under a landlord and the smallest average area of land under an owner farmer were cultivated. The rural society of England was thus divided into three parts—the revenue enjoying landlord, the grain merchant landlord, and the peasant community. But this rural society too slowly vanished and the English became urbanized. Wherever there were factories, there were crowds and there was the town.

Just as on the one hand it was capitalist agriculture, so too on the other hand it was the invention of new tools and machines and the vast wealth from colonial enterprises that was responsible for the total change in English society and the creation of a new class structure. A study of the inventions of tools and machines of this age seems to suggest that the inventors were not motivated by altruism. The coalmines were filling up with water and the water had to be quickly drawn out. The workers failed to do anything, a new device was required; uneducated engineers used their common sense and came up with a makeshift device. Later, an inventor modified these devices and created a new machine that could pump water out of the pits as well as send goods from one town to another at a faster and cheaper rate. By this method, machines came to be widely used in cotton mills, road laying, digging channels, transport systems, rails and ships. Of course all this was due to science. Granting the objections of today's scientists this science may be called applied science or technology. It is not that the use of machines only increased the volume and rate of production; it also changed the way of deriving livelihood from external Nature. The first change was in the means of production; machines in place of humans, from which man began to be alienated more and more, and as a result of which the social process of production became depersonalized and inhuman. The second change was in the form of social power. Earlier it was power to those who had more grain, now it was the one with money or the ability to borrow money who would have more power and more influence. Earlier the yardstick of social power had been nurturing, now power was delinked from social welfare and used only for increased production. Earlier those in power had a responsibility to society, now the strong were responsible only for their own economic gains and the application of strength was to establish the control of powerful individuals and powerful classes. For all this planning was needed, as also new machines, new markets, or else new levels of demand in the old markets, rationalism, and the intelligence to achieve aims, pragmatism, and a dedication to profit. The more the money accumulated, the more the machines increased, and the more the machines increased, the more the money accumulated—as though it were a natural law! Earlier, in the Middle Ages, one would have to go to the weaver's house for a piece of cloth, the weaver would not weave good cloth unless he received an order. A mill owner could not wait for such a personal order. The mill and the money had to be constantly employed; if made to wait they would, like the ghosts in fairy tales, kill off their master. Everything was cast in the same mould and produced in large quantities. Thus arose the need for division of labour, easy transportation, and unrestricted trade and commerce in new markets. These needs are the basic statement of the history of nineteenth century England. Spurred by these, England was transformed into today's British Empire.

Class division in the age of mills and factories is a major factor in social change. It has been stated earlier that the condition of those dependent on agriculture was worsening under the new feudal system. Cottage industry workers too declined in the competition from mills and factories. A new type of landlord and the factory owners—these two communities—merged and became transformed into the new rich class. Needless to say, this division of labour is of a new sort, but not a new creation. There was class division earlier, it exists now too, only the landlord and the tenant class now became the factory owner and the working class. The existence of class division in primitive times has been proved. Among the uncivilized, divisions between man and woman, child, youth and the aged, the authority and the ruled, and class divisions in respect of matrimony are historic facts. According to many this is not an economic division. Even if it were not so, it does not prove that as a result of having conquered external Nature, or having established some other relation to Nature, there was no economic class division among them. Alongside the biological division between man and woman, young and old, there was division of labour too. Let us assume that class division took place in the later part of the agricultural age. But then human beings were not aware of it. The first historical reason is perhaps this, that the Brahmins or the priestly class tried to keep it a secret with the help of religion itself. At this time the preacher of social unity was the priest and the beneficiary was the landlord and later the greatest landlord, that is the king. The king became the protector of religion, and the spiritual helmsman. No writing by a great author of this age reveals that society was not one but disparate. However, society was then indeed getting transformed into classes. At that time people were interested in small occupations rather than in the larger social set-up. But the fact that guilds or professions had been created in the middle ages is not the last word in the history of civilization. What was happening unobserved was the creation of a new class. Modern civilization is more closely linked to this than to the unity brought about by the Catholic Church. When it was seen that there was more profit in import and export of grains and other raw materials than in mere subsistence level farming, with the beginning of travelling by sea instead of by roads and paths, of small towns instead of villages, regular markets instead of fairs and makeshift market days, godowns in the city or by the river instead of the family granary in the courtyard, monetary transactions (later bills and cheques) instead of direct exchange, a group of gentlemen emerged who did not produce anything themselves but helped in trading produced goods. At first many of this group were Jews. There were reasons too, as due to initial religious restrictions Christians could not practice usury. That restriction was gradually softened due to Roman law. The history of that tempering too has been uncovered. At first the creditor could not charge any interest at all, he would get back only what he had lent. It was first decided according to Roman Law (*Damnum Emergens*) that if the creditor receives on the due date the amount he had lent, then he could receive a small extra amount for the risk of loss (loss that did not occur) taken by him. The creditor was all this while receiving an interest as loss risk, but furtively. What had been happening in secrecy earlier was now legitimized by law. And then *Lucrum Cessens*, that is the fact that the creditor had not engaged his money in business himself but given an opportunity to another to grow rich, was now recognized by law, and for his sacrifice the creditor became entitled to receive a portion of the borrower's profit. And then *Contractus Trinus*, that is, a contract between the creditor and the borrower against large sums and compensation for profit (It is suspected that the legal loopholes of the Middle Ages have now been transformed into the Austrian economists' opinions on interest and profit).

The outcome of the agricultural age is the feudal age—the class division in that society has been discussed earlier. But it has always to be kept in mind that it was in that age that the big banks were created in the trading cities of Italy and Germany. There, instead of the feudal landlords, the merchant and the moneylenders ran the administration of the city almost independently. They were the ones who sought permission from the government to trade in the colonies. The government too readily granted permission. At that time the King and his councillors and coterie were the government. Their need for money was then immense. Lots of goods began to arrive from the colonies then, gold and silver came from America. A new wealthy class emerged within the landlord community—the squirearchy, whose representative in England was Hampden. Under pressure of this class, the influence of the Roman Catholic Church, the feudal landlord, the priest and the king declined. In the words of those who interpret history in the light of religion, the system of Protestant rational ethics is the cause of the rise of this wealthy squire class! Even if their interpretation reverses the causal relationship, their account is mostly true. Where was the hunger in man's belly? Now, thanks to this squirearchy, production requirements were transformed to satiate pockets and mills, instead of man's hunger, and to hike up profit rates and seek new markets for unrestricted trade! On the one hand, men were grouping together, while on the other, the personal identity of the human being was vanishing. Everyone thought that this was Nature's law. Great scholars wrote books in order to understand this law of Nature; they even constructed a new code! These are the priests of the new rich. The economists, sages and pundits of India are the descendents of these persons. Adam Smith and Ricardo are the original propagators not only of economics but of individualism.

Even after the veneer of religion had come off, no opportunity was given for the class structure to be perceived by the people. A new whitewash was then applied - one was patriotism and the other liberalism, with which we are familiar, even though there is no corresponding Bengali word. This is not the place to write of these two approaches. I am merely assessing the nature of their internal relationship. The autocratic dominion established by the seventeenth century kings in Europe had found endorsement from the feudal landlord community. That was when patriotism came into existence. The sense of unity established by the Catholic religion was defeated at the hands of this patriotism. As a result of the pact between the king and the landlord community, the notion of physiocratism was preached. This did not have much currency in England. In England for the benefit of the newly rich, there was need for another concept, mercantilism. The English were the first to wake out of the enchantment of patriotism and the notion of one's own land. They first realized that there is no virtue nobler than liberalism. An assessment of this liberal view makes it obvious that it is nothing but the creation of the rich. It is through liberalism that the owners of factories demonstrate their utility, hide their selfish interests and bewitch others. After pursuing economic nationalism for almost a hundred years, it became necessary to prove that it was a hollow senseless thing. It was proved that the individual was at the root of society and that he had a few birthrights. He understands quite well what is good for him, therefore the world would benefit more if he were allowed to work in his own way. Therefore it was decided that there should not be any interference in individual liberty. Liberalism means individual liberty. Of course the individual does not mean just anybody but an individual of the wealthy business class. For other individuals tolerance was the greatest virtue because by being tolerant one would get food, not otherwise. There are many kinds of human beings in the world but since the inner essence of man is the same, it is no use quarrelling. Let all opportunities be given to that human essence, let equality, friendship and freedom triumph, let republicanism triumph! The essential man signifies that calculating creature whose job it is to buy cheap and sell at a high price, whose only application is the fulfilment of a particular target. (It is as a result of individualism that the force of intellectualism is heightened). The gist is, in order to conduct business it would not do to have any kind of obstacle; there should be no political obstacle, no tax obstacle nor the obstacle of distance. The money is there at home, in order to utilize that money, to convert raw materials into finished goods, markets are needed. The workers need freedom to take up jobs anywhere, to leave their land and homes and crowd at the gates of mills and factories. Whosoever objects at home will be thrown into prison; whosoever objects abroad will face war. That is, the market shall have no doors; the market will be unrestricted. Only one law will rule there. That law is not man made, it is God's, if not God's then Nature's, if not Nature's then human nature's, and if not even that then it should be so. That law is the profit motive. Great biologists, psychologists, philosophers, and economist stalwarts said, 'Yes, yes, that is indeed so, we have to come to that conclusion'. At once books were written. Professor Jogishchandra Sinha has recounted this history wonderfully in the pages of *Bichitra*.

England alone is not Europe. As the domination of feudalism prevailed in France and Germany for a longer period, the new class could not take shape there so early. The new class reared its head in France immediately after the French Revolution and in Germany almost fifty years later. In France it was because of small farmers being owners of land, the lack of coal and iron and the colonies changing hands that the squire class could not dominate the social and national structure. Germany was divided into many parts—the feudal landlord in one part and the small farmer in another, the mill and factory owners and merchants prevailing in between. Germany, moreover, did not even have a colony. It was for these reasons that the influence of the middle class was not experienced in France and Germany. Whatever little was, made France and Germany liberal to some extent during the initial phase of the Industrial Revolution. Compared to the present day there were fewer tariff restrictions on imported goods in those times.

But all nations cannot carry on unrestricted trade at the same time. Where is the market? There is no market apart from the different social segments within the country and the colonies outside. The patriotism created by the wealthy class raised objections to unrestricted trade and commerce with other nations. That is why there was pressure upon the rest of the world. Asia and Africa were divided. The product that yielded greater profit began to be produced in large quantities in one country. Yet there is no escape from competition. All countries were compelled to resort to novel scientific methods. The new version of labour division arose from this situation. Earlier within the country, society had the rich and the poor, owner and worker, industry and agriculture, now these divisions spread across the entire world. Europe took on the task of exporting finished goods and Asia, the colonies in Africa, and America supplied the raw material. In other words, the wealthy no more had something called homeland, and the creation of wealth helped workers do away with their geographical parameters. But some had more colonies, others less; some had more cargo ships, others less. Therefore the wealthy of the less fortunate nations turned their attention to their own countries. Earlier tariff had to be paid to send goods from one part of a country to another. That tariff was now removed. Roads, canals, and railways crisscrossed the country. Except for England and Holland, all the European nations now concentrated upon self-preservation, that is upon the unification of their own country. The state was God; nationalism was the strongest bond. This was the essence of German liberalism. English liberalism was very different. The basic principle of German liberalism was social and state unity, the basic principle of English liberalism was individual liberty. The reasons for the difference too are clear, the liberalism of England was the result of colonization and unrestricted trade. Germany's was a reaction to not having a colony. Perhaps that is the reason why Indians bred in the tradition of English thought do not really comprehend communism, fascism, and Nazism. The preachers of liberalism in Germany were philosophers such as Hegel and Fichte, an economist such as List, and an ethnologist such as Amon[?]. All of them respected history, that is, they arrived at their conclusions after considering the sequential and distinctive features of history. In Italy, Sismondi was the exponent of this theory. List saw that unrestricted global trade was not suitable for all nations. Some nations are agriculture based, some nations are trade and commerce based, therefore each country needs systems suited to its own conditions. List says that economic laws are historical and not natural. Unrestricted trade may take place only when all nations are on an equal footing. That is why the help of the government, of the state, is needed—because no other power in society can stop imports. Meanwhile let the production capacity of the state be made optimum as it was in England before the age of unrestricted trade, and as was then happening in America. A few things need to be noted in List's theory: (1) a regard for historical conditions and sequence, (2) economic nationalism, (3) dependence upon the state, (4) the impossibility of free trade for the time being. List was not against free trade. Rather he was in favour of it, though not for that time but for later, after the development of trade and commerce. After returning from America, List explained to his countrymen that free trade within the country could not take place unless geographical distances were conquered. It was on his advice that the railway network was expanded in Germany. On examination, List's basic theories seem to merely complement German capitalism. Seen from the other side too, it is natural that it appears so. List had learnt 'balanced economy' from America. He had realized that in order to achieve economic independence the state would have to strike a balance between agriculture and industry, and between those subsisting upon agriculture and those upon industry. No means of livelihood or no section of society could devour the other means or the other section. German workers had not come together as a class at that time, that is why 'means' denoted trade and commerce or agriculture, and 'class' denoted only government officials, traders and cultivators. These German (Prussian) landlords were like the seventeenth-century English landlords. They were masters and they were wealthy, their landholdings were vast, they ran their fiefdom with the aid of men and arms. They now asked help from the state according to List's propositions, for the transportation of food to all parts of the country. The state was forced to grant them many facilities. This is the basic fact of protectionism, that is, granting unrestricted freedom to the wealthy class, the trader and the landlord in the name of nationalism. The main aim of nationalism is to increase profit and create such a market where the cheap goods of another nation will not be allowed to enter. This freedom is the state's gift.

Now England took another path. The capitalism of England is older. The country too is smaller, all goods are not produced there, and it has to import goods for its entire year's food requirement, yet it has more money and more colonies. England has bought the world with cargo ships, life insurance, banks and other institutions. It is only expected that capitalism will easily become aggressive in such a situation. But the aggressive face is not to be revealed to others. The owners therefore, realizing the setbacks of competition, set up huge mills and factories. They founded monopolies on the strength of investments in the big establishments of the country, on the strength of science and on the strength of their rule in the colonies. The utility of the colonies across the oceans lay in conducting monopolistic trade. Today, that utility is everywhere about to die out; the wealthy class in the colonies has become a well wisher of the homeland. The reason behind a new flag in South Africa, is also the reason behind India's saffron flag. Despite many distinctions, this is where we are linked with the world. It is in this stream of history that our current history is developing and our minds and societies forming.

Three features prevail in our psychological history. One, the regular use of philosophical and religious terminology, two, nationalism, and three, liberalism. These three examples do not however express the essential thing about our history. Rather they conceal it. The Brahmin class, the Congress and the educated society are the protagonists of this secret conspiracy. The conspiracy of the Brahmin class is unexposed, despite being found out. Mahatmaji and Malviyaji are ready to give the untouchables access into the temple and the Council but they will not interfere with the four castes. The Chairman of the Untouchable Relief Society is one of the Birla brothers. The Congress itself does not know which side to please. Due to the counter currents of money on the one side and religion on the other, motivation is ending up in indifference (or *nishkam*), and emancipation (or *moksha*) is gradually receding. Whom shall the Congress satisfy, the businessman or the landlord? Whom does the agenda satisfy? The answer to this question itself exposes the agenda. The agenda of the wealthy class makes it appear that they have become aware of their historical role, that is why they are ready to help the Congress to some extent. The workers are not yet aware but it will perhaps not be very long before they are. On the one hand, the history of India is still going through the liberal age; on the other hand, all of us have to bear the consequences of the imperialism or domination that is impelled by the demands of monopolistic trade. There is an opposition between the two but that difference is in terms of pace and time lag. The opposition is not innate. Many believe that our society will very soon be split up into different segments due to outside pressure, just as a cell is quickly split up in the laboratory with the force of tremendous light.

The country expects much more from the educated class, whose ingratitude is without compare to have belied that expectation. That they were born in the refuge of foreign rulers and the wealthy is no respite for them. Of those who are most advanced among the educated class, their manifesto, that is their books, need to be read by all. Particularly those of the historians. Apart from a few they are all inspired by patriotism, all liberals of the English variety! None of them write social history. In none of their writings is explicated the nature of history or its methods. They have to depict causality but that depends only upon evidence. The substantiality of evidence is the only tool of their argument. They could have also been lawyers, but due to circumstances, perhaps because there was no big lawyer among their close kin, they have become historians. They are unacquainted with the experience and wisdom that works at the root and sequence of historical events. They do not write the history of social revolution. How society strives to survive, at which moment of crisis social formations change in order to survive better— these subjects they omit. They do not write the history of the common people. They ignore, perhaps even despise the common people. That is why our greatest historians are either lawyers in disguise or clerks in disguise. Their history writing is a dull repetition of clichéd stuff; it is neither contemporary history nor the history of the future. Whatever is happening, whatever has happened is good, to prove this is their aim.

There are many objections against the economists of India. We teach Adam Smith, Ricardo and Marshall, whose theories had been formed to endorse the unregulated and unrestricted trade of capitalism and imperialism. But in our hearts we want protectionism the nature of which too has been described in detail. What we teach and what we want are contradictory. Besides, we are against industrialism, and in favour of the *charka* and farming. But free trade and restricted trade, both relate to mills and factories. We have no acquaintance with countries that are agriculture based. We should study the histories of the Balkans and of Russia; we should know the history of the Green Revolution. Even in the universities, the histories of these countries are not taught. At the All India Economic Conference one is ridiculed if one discusses any view other than that of Marshall and his associates. That the All India Economic Conference is carrying on is because we have a familial unity, which is to support capitalist liberalism. Our economists had only looked at the interests of the wealthy class in the arguments of the Ottawa treaty. Those who objected did so considering the interests of Bombay traders or on the plea of patriotism; those who consented did so without comprehending the basic fact of British imperialism, that is opportunistic quest of monopoly trade. No one looked at social history. Upon this psychological framework of the Indian has been set science, philosophy and literature. That is why even a doctor of science is found to be conservative, and the demand for technical education instead of scientific education is constantly rising. The students of the science departments are in no way less superstitious than the students of the arts departments, that is why if they do not get government jobs they too proffer the advice that the science departments be shut down and colleges for technical education be set up, quoting the words of Acharya Prafulla Chandra. And philosophy! Our philosophy books are all histories of philosophy and that history too is compiled by sifting records. Literature today is in dire straits. The heroes and heroines of youthful literature all want to get rich, all want to climb socially. Whatever woe is depicted is the result of straitened means or else of problems of indulgence in romantic feelings.

This is the condition of our country. The distinctive feature here is—to live in the twentieth century and adopt the means of livelihood suited to eighteenth-century Europe. The question of good or ill luck does not arise here. The question is of historical trends and patterns where, though there is no play of the power of the supernatural, the invincible might of causality is in evidence.

8

History and Class Conflict

Earlier I have used the term 'class conflict'. In this chapter I shall try to explain the significance of 'class'. It is impossible to establish a definition here according to the laws of logic, since belief in class cannot be detached from the previous analysis of history and other beliefs. Belief in, rather than a definition of, history determines our course of action.

Belief is necessary for every kind of knowledge. Direct experience, when piecemeal, tends to be neglected. Perhaps the bits and pieces of experience are not connected with each other. Even when they are, the connection is not apparent. But from the point of view of knowledge, there is an urge to see experiences as linked with each other. This is accomplished by means of belief. When these experiences are strung and linked together, it is with the help of belief that our vision is extended and renewed. An extensive critique of such experiences is possible with the help of belief. By this means, the people in general can benefit from the knowledge of an individual. Belief is the language of the harmonization of knowledge and no one can claim a monopolistic right over language. Another aspect of belief is to establish a link between the environment, the person who possesses knowledge and knowledge which has been previously acquired. It is needless to discuss once again the state of antagonism which exists between knowledge and the one who possesses knowledge. However, we must stress the fact that unless this antagonism is removed, increase of knowledge is impossible, nor can the sage himself become a complete personality or gain peace by means of this knowledge. Only through belief can this antagonism be removed, thereby making possible the increase of knowledge and the development of a full

SUDESHNA CHAKRABORTY, Professor, Department of English, University of Calcutta, has translated 'History and Class Conflict' (originally titled 'Itihasa 3' or 'History 3', written in 1934–35).

personality. The task of creating leads to foresight. If it is the real aim of extended knowledge to enhance and control future experience with the help of an earlier understanding, then knowledge can never escape from belief.

Neither can history. From the point of view of the individual, it might be said that the wider historical belief helps past, present and even future experience to be linked together, in order to give the individual a fully rounded personality. It is this calculation which is the true point of view of the historian, true philosophy. The need for faith is felt all the more, in order to elevate certain kinds of knowledge to the level of science, and even a number of new kinds of faith are needed. The knowledge that is being discussed here is history, whose content consists of a tradition or stream of social experiences. This stream of course has its rules, since the experience happens to be a human experience and human activities do not take place wholly at random. On the other hand, there is the struggle and interaction with external nature. Thanks to science, the laws of external nature are more organized and well defined than those of human nature. That is, some parts of the contents of history are more regulated by science than others. A particular event in external nature might be detached from the general chain of events, turned into an abstraction, without socially harming the scientist in any way. But no experience in human nature can be freed from continuity, since this continuity is not mechanical. It consists of a synthesis of what comes before and after, and any attempt at separation harms man socially. Because of these two reasons, among others, external events can be reconstituted in laboratories, while the cluster of internal events cannot be replicated. (All this is, of course, relative). Numbers constitute a general quality of class and its other qualities are made possible by the repetition of a particular quality. (Here by class I mean the word 'class' as used in mathematical laws). Thus physical science is regulated by the rules of mathematics, and its success lies in this very subservience. On the other hand, psychology and sociology cannot be completely subordinate. They might indeed be subordinate to statistics, but subordination to mathematics would mar their success. The difference between the two sciences mentioned above is well known to all.

There cannot be too much argument on the question as to whether man-related sociology can ever take, or should take, the form of a science relating to external nature, such as physics. For the very means that is used for settling an argument is at present being subjected to the judgment of logic. Besides, scientific society has various faults as well as various good qualities. Thus, though perhaps sociology can be soon raised to the level of physics by adopting the scientific method completely, yet it is doubtful whether this would help to regulate the future progress of society. A scientific society might be such that the reconstruction of a new society by some individual or non-scientific force might become inevitable and necessary. It is better not to make such a prophecy, I am stating what I want to say right at the beginning—if we want to turn the partially true laws of society (general tendencies or direction of events) into a more complete truth, then for the time being it is better to adopt the means by which wider scientific truth has been discovered. This means the scientific method, which while not flawless, is very beneficial. And from the point of view of knowledge, the history of the scientific method is the history of belief. However history is not physics, and the belief inherent in physics or chemistry is not the belief of history.

I am considering physics the representative of the natural sciences. The difference between the nature of physics and the nature of history cannot be denied. In my opinion, there are three basic differences: (1) Physics is independent of geographical location and especially, of time. The structure of a nuclear particle is the same in India and Holland. What it is today, it was many centuries ago and will remain the same a hundred years hence. Only opinions might change. On the other hand, history is time and place specific. Of course, these specifications are not immutable decrees of fate, but rather, subject to certain rules. (2) The data of the subjects of physics have been directly derived from observation. Statements about them have been tested and are always ready to be subjected to further tests. Everything about physics is direct, tangible. In history, specifications are very few. History must be derived from the past or contemporary narrations of events that have happened, documents, stone inscriptions and the like. Only these signs can be directly observed. The rest of the work of a historian consists of indirect reconstruction, made somewhat in the manner of a jury or a detective. The historical method is mainly deductive. A historian does not know which event is true, which is false and which is exaggerated. He has to discover the truth. (Here the word 'history' has been used to indicate the narration of past events and their continuity.) We cannot say, 'All facts are born free and equal', since discipline and fetters do not possess the same importance. Rather, the time and space specific events that can be known through the method mentioned above should be considered historical events. It should always be remembered that the knowledge of a historian is indirect and of a deductive nature. (3) To the extent that the deductive method or inversion is used in physics, it is pure and unmixed. No new event is allowed to enter it. Rather, any such event is discarded as irrelevant. This is not possible in the case of history. In history, the number of events which come uninvited is not small and they must be accorded at least a verbal welcome. Because of this, the deductive method of history is impure, mixed. That is to say, the causality which exists in the assembly of historical events must accommodate mental processes, such as the nature, will and aim of man. The influence of sudden events in the natural world too, cannot be ignored. There is a place for the sudden, the unexpected in history, like mutation in the evolutionary theory of life. The extent of this place is not the subject of this article. However, the acknowledgement of the accidental is bound to dilute the purity of the deductive method. The knowledge of this fact can help us to understand the difference between history and physics as regards nature and methodology.

Because of the above-mentioned reason, belief in history is bound to be different from the belief involved in physics. Belief in physics is relatively free, abstract, detached from, even though derived from, the subject matter. They [the beliefs] are disembodied inhabitants of an imaginary world. They resemble a mannequin parade in some large dress shop, watched by astonished people from outside the glass window. In the incomparable words of Bradley, they are like a troupe of bloodless dancing girls on the stage. But historical beliefs consist of flesh and blood. They are embodied, united, not free from the use specified by time and place. All beliefs are imaginary, yet historical beliefs seem part of the real world. They seem even closer to the ordinary people, without much of a barrier. Because it is linked to social behaviour, the assembly of subjects, in the case of historical beliefs, is spread over a long stretch of time. Belief related to physics is always timeless. Natural events can be simplified by being brought into the laboratory, but not historical events. They remain complex and varied. Therefore belief as regards physics has to be built up through a process of rejection, finalized through negative judgment. On the other hand, while the subject of history can be known indirectly, historical belief is, relatively speaking, derived from direct knowledge. If it is rejected its existence becomes of a different nature. In other words, it ceases to exist at all. This is rather like the policy of cooperation and non-cooperation. Historical belief is more dynamic and regulates our work. If we become conscious about faith in physics, the laws of nature cannot be changed, nor can nature be diverted to a different path. Only science advances. However, it is possible to bring about social change and progress with the help of faith in history, that is, by becoming conscious of it. The succession of historical events is like a continuous flow. Succession in physics is a definite series, like the photographic reels of a film. The past in history comes alive in the present and provides the present with premonitions of the future. Like a snowball, it increases as it goes along, the earlier part entering, at least partially, into the later part. Therefore there must be evaluation within historical belief, but such a process in the case of belief in physics would be disastrous. Of course, these differences are relative. With increase in knowledge, the difference will decrease, but I do not know whether a historian will be ever able to discard moral judgment and a code of values. For while the physicist is a man, man is not his subject. On the other hand, a historian, even if he is acting as a detective or a jury is a man and his subject is also man. In this case, it is very difficult for a historian to do without a code of values. A man might wish to turn another man into a machine or a number, but he would not wish a similar transformation for himself. It is true that if a code of values is based on absolutely true events then the historian need not be ruthlessly impersonal like other scientists, without harming the scientific method. Love for truth is at the root of science and this can hardly be considered opposed to a sense of values.

Class and conflict are parts of the historical faith mentioned above. Later, I shall discuss the issue of conflict. The word class indicates two mental states. (1) A sense of unity and equality among people belonging to the same class. Because of a shared mental state and unity, mutual sympathy is born within a limited space; this might be called feeling of kind rather than consciousness of kind, for a conscious state of affairs does not always exist but might appear at a later stage. (2) A clear or vague idea of being superior or inferior in relation to beings of another class. These feelings consist of many feelings, since there are not just one or two high and low strata. Society is divided into several classes, yet every class touches another one way or another. These feelings depend on education, way of life, mutual acquaintance, near or distant relations, many kinds of social, political and financial inequality. Such, according to Morris Ginsberg, is the meaning of class. In his opinion, there is no need to put forward any aim or interest in order to define a class, since very few classes are clearly conscious of aims or interests. Needless to say, while this explanation fits in with sociology, it is not consistent with the way we have been trying to understand history. 'We belong to the same party' is a sentiment not detached from historical events. Such a sentiment has been mostly created and sustained by financial reasons. Its basic existence depends on a conscious or unconscious state. A class is born when aims or interests, centred round the right of production, build up a human collective. Production, like class, is a very old concept. The process and right of production, like the nature of classes, are changing. However, classes remain, as do production and rights. The frontiers of a class are determined by the limits of interests. They constantly create obstacles since the forces of production in the same society, at the same time, are not so abundant as to be divided equally and satisfy all parties. Certainly they cannot, as long as property relations in the whole of society are clearly defined by the state, and as long as property belongs to individuals rather than to the people in general, that is as long as rights remain differentiated. Moreover, the knowledge to carry out discoveries and opportunities to use such discoveries in order to increase the forces of production are not evenly distributed among all classes. Therefore seeds of conflict are bound to exist among classes. With the increase of conflict, a class becomes more firmly knit. The significance of conflict is to bring the means of production under control, that is, establish mastery over other classes. On the individual level, establishment of mastery means leadership. But even if biological differences lie at the root of this master–slave relationship, its eternal permanence is due to economic inequality. The master is always reluctant to abdicate, so mastery must always be based on illiberal force and coercion. Besides, every kind of mastery includes hopes of gain. It is the hope of profit that drives a class. For this reason a class can never fully realize what is beneficial for the people. The benefit that a particular class seeks is partial. The truth is that social practice and contemporary action consist of conflict and truce, mastery and slavery, gain and loss, social welfare and class interest. These eternal currents in opposite directions should be observed by historians. Class belief is a scientific belief in such cross-currents. Though this belief implies conflicts, belief in conflict, according to many, is far more extensive. Conflict is the law of the universe. When this law takes on a human manifestation through history class becomes the refuge of this conflict, which might then be defined as class conflict. In my opinion, class and conflict are not wholly separate concepts.

According to more than one scholar, belief in class is meaningless, because this cannot be separated from categories related to caste, vocation or profession and craft. I am unwilling to accept this point of view, since class in the sense mentioned above, can easily be so separated. There is more than one class in society, they are mingled together, an individual can belong to more than one collective. These two are not really objections but obstacles in the way of establishing a belief in class. Caste is a tradition fostered since birth which, till date, has been validated by religion. There is no place for a religious tradition in the concept of class. At best it can be seen as a coating. Even if eugenics does not prove the existence of castes or justify the class system, by virtue of figures it can be said that there are qualitative divisions within society. It is true that in history and contemporary society, class and qualitative, statistical divisions are not identical. No branch of learning other than magic proves that the Brahmin community occupies the highest place and the Sudras the lowest, as regards intelligence and character. The same thing can be said about foreign countries, where classes, grown old, have almost ossified into castes. Today, in Hindu society, caste is merely a religious belief. While the influence of economic and material interests plays a role within the caste system, it is veiled by a religious and spiritual tradition. Caste was created to hold, with the help of certain spiritual beliefs, a special place in society. Yet, looking at the matter from outside, it might seem as if such a position and honour was automatic. It goes without saying that this is not so, and nothing is decided automatically. The power that determines social position is the history and expression of the social process known as production, the relationship between the collective of producers and other collectives in society, that is to say, the right to property and the means of earning an income. The appearance and development of this force is thwarted by religious tradition and practice. The nature of history is obscured in the same way. It is through belief in class that this force can attain its full development and the nature of history be fully revealed.

There are many kinds of vocations, crafts and professions, such as medicine, law, engineering, etc. In our ancient history there were classes and communities. The first was a group of businessmen who traded among themselves, and the second denoted a professional group needing the help of more than one businessman. Today, all traces of these people are on the verge of disappearing. We might perhaps find them in places such as Indore and Madurai, but their roots have withered away. These classes have no basic connection with class in the sense that we have used the term. They had been living until now, covered by the weeds of tradition. After removing the weeds it has been discovered that they are dead. Tradition-based castes, at the beginning, were moved in a way by the forces of production. This force became divided according to the division of labour, ability and convenience of apprenticeship and created vocation. This force has likewise played a role in dividing a caste into many, or in uniting many castes. The forces that today lead to caste creation or division cannot be traced to economics. Rather, they might be found in the history of religious tradition and the greed for political gain. However, the real story is different, though it has not yet become apparent. Today, thanks to British rule, the method of producing goods for the market has at least changed in India. Society is not able to contain these new forces, just as old bottles cannot contain new wine. Therefore society is in the throes of revolution. The conflict between the contained and the container has created opportunities for the real development of classes. Perhaps new classes have not yet been created, since this conflict is a civil dissension, rather than a true conflict, mostly sound and fury. Even if new classes have risen they are not yet conscious of their own role in the historical background. It is as if, in the absence of an actor, one of the audience has been called to the stage. He is anxious to win fame in the theatre, yet is nervous and has received assurance about adequate prompting. But how far can prompting alone carry him? Particularly when the opposing side too, has forgotten its dialogue. We are all acquainted with this state of affairs, so certain errors are permissible. Now I wish to state, that whether in Hindu or European society or even in China, the position of castes, craft based classes and communities sharing the same profession used to be determined according to methods of production. In a mainly agricultural society crafts catered mostly to the consumption demands of the fashionable section in society, as an extra appendage to farm work. There would have been no production without demand. At that time, only the community of landlords was conscious of its existence, work and aims. They alone constituted a class in our sense of the word. Now, however, the process of production has changed, even though the nature and appearance of property have remained the same. The number of craftsmen is no longer insignificant. With the increase in numbers, many of the traditional qualities of these groups have been lost. They used to be artists and specialists. However, as their number increased, physical strength for labour replaced artistic talent. Common sense and quickness were substituted for specialized knowledge. Nowadays, almost everywhere, the vocation of a worker has become the most important one, surpassing all others. Agriculture is less profitable, while cottage industries have been destroyed. The working classes do not have to understand whether there is demand or not. Their only duty is to work. The masters are supposed to understand everything. Even so, calculations go wrong and there is over production. Today, in reality, it is the machines that are in direct demand. Machines must be kept functioning to avoid disaster. It is the machine that is now the master of the worker. Besides, the vocations mentioned above depended on manual labour. The crafts were traditional and the traditions were not subject to change through scientific experiments. Only slight changes were brought about slowly, very slowly, through the experience acquired through manual labour, while respecting tradition. Today, thanks to science, new machines are being made every day. The experience of workers and craftsmen is being devalued, since there is little opportunity for the application of such experience in wider fields. Division of labour and specialization are increasing rapidly. The vast masses of workers do not know science and cannot carry out scientific experiments. They lack the opportunity of acquiring higher learning. The master class believes that workers are fit only for manual labour, not for education. Proofs of this theory appear in the books of learned professors, and the science of eugenics seems to point in a similar direction. Moreover, higher education is excessively expensive. All institutes of higher education are in the hands of professionals. These institutes have been financed by wealthy people, landlords and mill owners. Therefore, only their children will become scientists and join the prestigious professions.

This is a description of the contemporary situation. Meanwhile, a new class is emerging, amidst the greatest secrecy. It is called profession. In the case of crafts, the conversion to physical labour is preceded by the formation of a group of specialists. Their brain simplified manual work or craftsmanship, that is, increased the alienation of the division of labour. Thick rubber can be thinned by pulling it, but too great a pull is likely to tear it altogether. That is why the upper limit of the profession, that is the learned scholars, have become detached from the body of society. Society today is headless. The scholars have discarded aims geared to social practice and, in revenge, society has discarded them. The most ridiculous side of the present turning point of time is this: the national leaders are acting in a way that is diametrically opposed to what the scholars are saying. The scholars want free trade or peace in trade. In reality, exactly the opposite is taking place. Tariff walls are growing higher and higher, conflicts are increasing. Because of an excessive division of labour, the social link between intelligence and work, science and the applied crafts, opinions and action, intellectuals and the working masses has been destroyed. That is why the rich have established complete control over those who are mere workers. This is the historical role of the professions—they have contributed to the growth of science and specialized knowledge, and, on the other hand, the result of their work has led to the deterioration of the conditions of the workers. The same deed can bring about good and bad results—such is the law of historical destiny. Only knowledge can liberate us from the grip of this destiny. In this case, it would be natural to suppose that each profession constitutes a class. This is because, even while enhancing the forces of production, they have not established ownership over the means of production and have remained satisfied with only a small share of the social wealth. That, too, simply as fees. For their lack of desire is balanced by the excessive desire of another class. Today the tribes of specialists are nothing but the obedient servants of this class. Moreover, they are not conscious of the results of their own action. Their faith is, 'never think of the fruits of your work.' We must hesitate to call these *jnan-yogis* a class. The nature of a class is that of *karma yoga*.

The history of professions in Europe has been reconstructed. In the beginning, a few businessmen in their leisure hours, in the interval of social intercourse and pleasure, used to discuss their business affairs. Later, they demanded an income that was commensurate with their status as gentlemen. Nor were their demands groundless. Their long apprenticeship has enriched their experience, on the basis of which they have acquired specialized knowledge, which in turn, has benefited society. They are in possession of a special methodology of knowledge and they alone, no one else, are skilful in the application of this technique. This is the history of professions, according to Carr-Saunders. I am quoting a few lines from the new book of Whitehead: 'Profession means a vocation whose activities are subjected to theoretical analysis and modified by theoretical conclusions derived from that analysis'.

In other words, foresight will be based on theory, and theory on experience derived from vocation. According to Sidney Webb, every profession is inspired by creative power, rights and consciousness of property and sympathy. Perhaps this opinion is not particularly valuable since these three kinds of trends are at the root of almost every group. It is not possible, with their help, to distinguish class from profession. I have already pointed out the fault and incompleteness of the two other concepts. However, I have quoted these two concepts simply to show that the special nature of professions have become apparent even to historians and sociologists holding different opinions. The professions in India are quite clearly created and sustained for the sake of spreading the political domination of a class of wealthy foreigners.

Therefore we accept the following views about class. (1) A community grows, centred around the forces of production, (2) Every community is linked with a process of production, defined by history; production is a social process and these relations are generally fixed by the state and sanctioned by law. (3) After the establishment of such a relationship, social labour and property are divided among this community. Later, the state proclaims this division to be eternal. Such a human collective is defined as a class. Therefore, in the scheme of historical progress, class occupies a special place. It is due to class conflicts that society has attained its present shape. If history is to have any link with the present, aside from going through old documents, if history is a contemporary narration, both giving hints of and regulating the future, if history is not a repetitive narrative but a dynamic one determining present action, then belief in class has to be accepted in this sense and class conflict acknowledged as the chief force behind historical progress. (4) The best way of firmly knitting together a community is conflict. (5) The nature of conflict is hope of profit and establishing domination over the centres of production. In other words: 'Classes are groups of people, such that one group may appropriate to itself the toil of the other owing to the difference of their (historic) situation, which is itself determined by the mode of their economic life' (Julius F. Hecker, *Moscow Dialogues*). (6) A class cannot exist unless it is conscious of itself. Without consciousness of class conflict, radical social change cannot be brought about. Needless to say, all promises are built around a core formula. (7) Many believe that classes have other roots, besides economic and historical ones, such as religious and social traditions, state rules and customs. Since political reasons are always present within conflicts, they have been already included in our concepts. Education, opportunities and other social reasons for class divisions are mainly economic. The divisions based on religious traditions are not class divisions. Often, traditional differences hinder or conceal the formation of class divisions. But the existence of these reasons cannot be denied. They are there and flourishing. Their base is firm enough but it must not be forgotten that the foundation of this monument is also economic.

In the last chapter, I have described the old history of classes. In this chapter, I am explaining an idea that is extremely necessary for understanding the nature of past and of contemporary history. Only someone who is perfectly aware of the future of scientific production can venture to predict the future of classes. But from the point of view of logic, it can be said that if a sense of private property, monopoly over production and selfishness decrease, the field of conflict will narrow down and at the same time classes will become more extensive, spreading throughout society. The frightening intensity of class conflicts will then diminish. Conflicts will persist in one form or another, for perhaps progress through obstacles and conflicts is the law of the universe. The end of all conflicts will signify the end of the world. The only social duty of the historian is to employ this universal force consciously, in order to remove class differences. This is a duty not only on behalf of society, but also on behalf of the individual. For it is due to class difference that man is unable to attain full humanity. Yet this was inevitable. Society has developed, and will continue to do so, through the expression, overcoming and synthesis of all the inconsistencies, imbalances, disparities, conflicts and contradictions that are inherent in it. When a particular community carries out this task consciously, it is known as class conflict. This is the true significance of class conflict. I know that in this chapter a concept according to the laws of logic has not been established. The way we have tried to understand history is not consistent with logical concepts. Our belief will guide us, help us to go forward and indicate our goal.

Glossary

Babbitt. The novel *Babbitt* by Sinclair Lewis was published in 1922. It depicts the complacency and materialism of George F. Babbitt, a real-estate broker and representative middle-class family man from the city of Zenith in the American Midwest. Babbittry has become a byword for the superficial values of business culture.

Bakunin, Mikhail Aleksandrovich (1814–1876). Prominent Russian revolutionary anarchist and a prolific political writer. His differences with Karl Marx split the European revolutionary movement for a long time. Although his voluminous writings are often incomplete and rambling, he inspired a large and widespread following by the force of his personality.

Bauer, Otto (1881–1938). A theoretician of the Austrian Social Democratic Party who suggested the creation of nation-states to solve the problem of nationalities of the Austro-Hungarian Empire. According to him, the conflict between nationalities is essentially a class struggle. Bauer was the founder of the socialist educational movement *Die Zukunft* (The Future). After World War I, he became one of the principal advocates of Austria's unification with Germany.

Berkeley, George (1685–1753). An Anglo-Irish Anglican bishop and an empiricist philosopher who believed that everything which is not spiritual exists only in so far as it is perceived, or is capable of being perceived, by the senses. His philosophy of immaterialism stood on two premises: (a) that there is the active mind perceiving, thinking and willing; and (b) that there are passive objects that the mind apprehends, viz. sensory data and imaginable ideas.

Blanqui, Louis-Auguste (1805–1881). A revolutionary socialist, Blanqui was a legendary figure of French radicalism who suffered imprisonment for more than thirty-three years in all. As a theoretician of revolution, he believed in the inevitability of class struggle, and the need in the socialist transformation of society for a temporary dictatorship which would bring industrial and commercial enterprises under state control. In the following stage, the formation of associations of agricultural and industrial production and fostering of education would, he thought, empower the people to organize the country's economy to their own benefit.

Bradley, Francis Herbert (1846–1924). English idealist philosopher who was in opposition to the empiricist theories of thinkers such as John Stuart Mill and who pointed out the drawbacks of Mill's theory of Utilitarianism. Bradley drew from Hegel's ideas and held that mind was a more fundamental feature of the universe than matter. His best known work is *Appearance and Reality: A Metaphysical Essay* (1893), which is valued especially for its sharp dialectic and rigorous search for truth.

Brahma's *Muhurta Parikalpana*. *Muhurta* is a moment or any short space of time or, specifically, one-thirtieth part of a day. *Kalpa* is a day of Brahma or a thousand *Yugas* or a period of four thousand three hundred and twenty million years of mortals.

Brahma's *Yoga* slumber. Brahma or the Supreme Being is supposed to indulge in *Yoganidra* or the sleep of meditation for aeons.

Burke, Edmund (1729–1797). As a British statesman and a political thinker, Burke was more concerned with the curtailment of the crown's power than with parliamentary reforms. In respect of the American colonies, he advocated a pragmatic and conciliatory approach. In respect of India, he condemned the corruption and lack of justice inherent in the activities of the East India Company in particular, and British governance in general. It was at his instigation that Warren Hastings was impeached in 1787. Burke's hostile views on the French Revolution provoked Thomas Paine to write *The Rights of Man* (1791–92).

Carr-Saunders, Sir Alexander (Morris) (1886–1966). Sociologist, demographer and director of the London School of Economics and Political Science, University of London from 1937 to 1956. He is widely known for his contribution to historical studies in demography and for his work in establishing university colleges overseas such as in Khartoum, Kuala Lumpur, in East and West Africa, and in the West Indies.

Cassirer, Ernst (1874–1945). A German-Jewish philosopher best known for his interpretation of cultural values. Building on the work of Immanuel Kant, Cassirer extended Kant's principles to include developments that had taken place since the time of Kant. Cassirer argued, on the basis of his analysis of various forms of man's cultural expression, that man is unique in his ability to use the symbolic forms of myth, language and science for structuring his experiences and understanding both himself and the world of nature. His *Essay on Man* (1944) is an introduction to the philosophy of human culture.

Condorcet, Jean Antoine Nicolas Caritat, Marquis de (1743–1794). French philosopher of the Enlightenment—a Philosophe—famous for his advocacy of educational reform. Author of *Sketch for a Historical Picture of the Progress of the Human Mind* (1795), Condorcet was a champion of many causes such as economic freedom, religious toleration, legal and educational reform, and abolition of slavery. He sought to establish the supremacy of reason in social affairs. His explanation of human behaviour was of a kind that anticipated the discipline of sociology.

Dawson, Christopher (1889–1970). English Catholic historian, a man of vast erudition and a prolific writer. His research on the history and institutions of the Christian religion led him to challenge prevalent assumptions about culture and history, denounce the Western religion of progress and assert the need to recover the spiritual tradition at the root of the culture of Western Europe. Some of his well known books are *Progress and Religion* (1929), *Religion and the Modern State* (1936), *Dynamics of World History* (1957) and *The Crisis of Western Education* (1961).

Durkheim, Emile (1858–1917). French social scientist and author of *The Division of Labour in Society* (original French edn 1893) and *Suicide* (original French edn 1897) who developed a methodology combining empirical research with sociological theory. Durkheim did not think of science and technology as necessarily leading to progress. In fact, he said, mechanization endangers social and ethical structures by fostering 'anomie' and rootlessness. Durkheim helped to define the subject matter of sociology and establish it as a discipline.

Edgeworth, Francis Ysidro (1845–1926). Irish economist and statistician who applied mathematics to his areas of study and contributed to theories of international trade, taxation and monopoly. His best known work is *Mathematical Physics* (1881), in which he introduced concepts which later became standard devices of economic theory.

Fechner, Gustav Theodor (1801–1887). German physicist and philosopher, and founder of the science of psychophysics. Fechner developed procedures which are still useful in experimental psychology, such as measuring sensations in relation to the physical magnitude of the stimuli producing them.

Fichte, Johann Gottlieb (1762–1814). German philosopher and one of the great transcendentalist Idealists. He was influenced by Kant's doctrine of the inherent moral worth of man. The philosophy of Fichte during his residence at Jena is marked by its ethical emphasis, while the period in Berlin saw the emergence of a mystical and theological theory of Being. Among his friends were the leading lights of German Romanticism: Friedrich Schlegel, August Wilhelm Schlegel and Friedrich Schleiermacher.

Fromm, Erich (1900–1980). German-born American psychoanalyst and social philosopher who explored the interaction between psychology and society. He deplored the fact that modern man had become alienated from himself in the consumerist industrial society, and called for a new enlightenment in the new society in which the individual would be able to fulfil his personal needs while preserving the bonds of social brotherhood. Fromm's writings on human nature, ethics and love are not just for social scientists but for a wide general readership.

Ginsberg, Morris (1889–1970). British sociologist of Lithuanian–Jewish descent. After a distinguished academic career in London, Ginsberg succeeded L.T. Hobhouse (his teacher, with whom he co-authored *The Material Culture and Social Institutions of the Simpler Peoples*, published in 1915) to the Martin White Professorship at the London School of Economics in 1930. His major works are *The Psychology of Society* (1920), *Studies in Sociology* (1932), *Sociology* (1934) and *Reason and Unreason in Society* (1947).

Godwin, William (1756–1836). Social philosopher, political journalist and religious dissenter. Godwin's discourse of aestheticism, anarchism, and individual liberty in his writings anticipated English Romanticism. His thought was a combination of cultural determinism with a doctrine of extreme individualism. His principal work, *An Enquiry Concerning Political Justice and its Influence on General Virtue and Happiness* (1793), was a rejection of conventional government with its recourse to tyrannical manipulation.

Hampden, John (1594–1643). English Parliamentary leader opposed to King Charles I on the question of ship money. He also vigorously attacked other royal policies and took part in the English Civil War, in which he was fatally wounded in a skirmish with Royalists.

Harrison, Frederic (1831–1923). English Positivist philosopher who was instrumental in promoting August Comte's Positivism in Great Britain. He founded, along with Richard Congreve, the Church of Humanity in London based on Positivist philosophy. He is the author of *Positivism: Its Position, Aims and Ideals* (1901), *The Philosophy of Common Sense* (1907) and *The Positive Evolution of Religion* (1913).

Hebert, Jacques-Rene (1757–1794). A political journalist, Hebert was the chief spokesman for the Parisian sansculottes in the revolutionary period in France. His supporters, the Hebertists, organized massive demonstrations of Parisian workers and forced the initiation of a state-controlled economy. Anti-Christian campaigns seeking to destroy Roman Catholic institutions were also largely inspired by Hebert. Although he had joined the Club of Jacobins, his extremism came under attack from right-wing Jacobins and he was guillotined in March 1794. But his execution cost the Jacobin regime the support of the sansculottes and led to its collapse in July 1794.

Huberman, Leo (1903–1968). Founding co-editor, with Paul M. Sweezy, of the magazine *Monthly Review*, which, along with the Monthly Review Press, became a forum of independent Marxian socialism in the United States in the first half of the twentieth century. Huberman was involved in a radical progressive education movement in an effort to place children at the centre of education, imparting to them not only knowledge but also the ability to inquire, understand and make decisions about their own lives. *We the People* (1932) is his pathbreaking history of the United States from the point of view of its working people. His other works are *Man's Wordly Goods: The Story of the Wealth of Nations* (1936), *America Incorporated* (1940) and *The ABC of Socialism* (1953)—the last co-authored with Sybil May.

Huxley, Sir Julian (1887–1975). Grandson of eminent biologist Thomas Henry Huxley and eldest brother of Aldous Huxley. Known best as a zoologist, Sir Julian conducted scientific research in areas such as hormones, developmental processes, ornithology and ecology. He was the first director general of UNESCO (1946–48). Apart from many works on evolution and other scientific subjects, Sir Julian wrote on his view of humanism in essays which were collected and published as *Essays of a Humanist* (1964).

Korzybski, Alfred (1879–1950). Born and educated in Warsaw, Korzybski went over to North America in 1916 and became a US citizen in 1940. He founded a discipline which he called general semantics, not to be confused with semantics, which he outlined in *Science and Sanity: An Introduction to Non-Aristotelian Systems and General Semantics* (1933). An important premise of Korzybski's theory is encapsulated in his famous dictum 'the map is not the territory', a principle which has also influenced work in the area of neuro-linguistic programming.

Kropotkin, Peter (1842–1921). Born into the Russian aristrocacy and an accomplished geographer, Kropotkin became a theorist of 'anarchic communism'. He wrote many influential works, among them *Mutual Aid* (1902), in which he showed that cooperation was more important than conflict in the evolution of species. Kropotkin envisaged a society on the lines of a co-operative community in which members would do mental and manual work in the prime years of their life, and would draw from the common store as much as they needed.

List, Friedrich Georg (1789–1846). German-born American economist who advocated tariff protection to stimulate national industrial development. His best known works are *Outline of American Political Economy* (1827) and *The National System of Political Economy* (1841).

Ludendorff, Erich (1865–1924). Prussian general and military strategist who was appointed chief of staff of the German Eighth Army in World War I, to combat the might of the Russian army in eastern Prussia. Extremely ambitious, he claimed that he had been the real commander of World War I and that the war was lost because of sabotage by the home-front. He had a major role in directing reactionary political movements after the war, and finally joined the Nazi Party.

mansabdari. The ownership of land bestowed to army commanders. In India *mansabdars* were graded imperial officials of the Mughal Empire, but their offices and estates were not hereditary.

Marshall, Alfred (1842–1924). One of the chief proponents of classical economics in the tradition of Adam Smith, Ricardo and John Stuart Mill. Professor of Political Economy in Cambridge from 1885 to 1908, Marshall authored several books which are an important contribution to economic literature: *The Pure Theory of Foreign Trade* (1879), *The Principles of Economics* (1890), *Industry and Trade* (1919), *Money, Credit and Commerce* (1923).

Maxwell, James Clerk (1831–1879). Great Scottish physicist best known for his formulation of electromagnetic theory, Maxwell has had an electromagnetic unit named in his honour. Einstein spoke of his work as 'the most profound and the most fruitful that physics has experienced since the time of Newton'.

Michelson, Albert Abraham (1852–1931). German-born American physicist who established the speed of light as a fundamental constant and was awarded the Nobel Prize for Physics in 1907. Michelson collaborated with E.W. Morley in what is known as the Michelson–Morley experiment. The results of the experiment, announced in 1887, were negative, for the scientists failed to detect any 'ether-drag' effect on the speed of light or any motion of the earth relative to ether. It was a significant experiment, however, leading to Albert Einstein's formulation of the theory of relativity in 1905.

Minkowski, Hermann (1864–1909). German mathematician whose major work was based on the idea of a four-dimensional space, combining the three dimensions of space with that of time. This idea provided the mathematical foundation for Einstein's general theory of relativity.

Mir. A self-governing community of peasants in the history of Russia. The Mir was retained even after the abolition of slavery in 1861 as a system of communal land tenure and an organ of local administration.

moksha. Emancipation from desire and thus emancipation from the cycle of worldly woes. This is also the essential tenet of Buddhism. The author has used this religious term ironically in the seventh essay to underline the basic contradiction of Hindu philosophy with individualism and liberal capitalism.

Monosha. Manasa Devi—in Bengali pronunciation *Manasa* becomes *Monosha*—was originally an *adivasi* or tribal goddess who was later included in the Hindu pantheon. Manasa is worshipped today mainly in Bengal as a snake goddess who also protects human beings from snake bites. The *Manasa Mangal Kavya* depicts the story of her relentless persecution of the merchant Chand who refused to worship any deity except Siva. Manasa planned to attack Chand's son Lakhinder on his wedding night by entering, through a hole, the metal chamber that the father had built for the newly-weds, and succeeded after many attempts.

Morley, Edward Williams (1838–1923). American chemist who collaborated with the physicist A.A. Michelson in the Michelson–Morley experiment. See Michelson above.

nishkam. The lack of personal desire advocated for action in Hindu philosophy as expounded in the *Gita*; used ironically in the seventh essay.

Nyaya. One of the six orthodox systems of Indian philosophy ascribed to the sage Gotama or Gautama. *Nyaya* means 'going into' a subject, or analysis. It is concerned primarily with logical processes and the laws of thought, as well as with epistemology. It is also called *Tarkavidya* or the science of reason, and *Vadavidya* or the science of discussion. *Nyaya* is classed together with another school of philosophy, the *Vaiseshika*, and the two are called the Atomic School.

Ola Debi. Known as *Ola Devi* to Hindus and *Ola Bibi* to Muslims, she is the goddess of cholera and was worshipped widely in West Bengal and Bangladesh until her importance was reduced by the decreased incidence of the disease.

Physiocratism. The ideas of a group of social reformers and theorists headed by Francois Quesnay in eighteenth-century France. Physiocratism was characterized by the belief that agriculture is the only source of wealth and that government policy should not interfere with natural economic laws. The term *laissez faire* was originally taken up by the Physiocrats.

Purana. The *Puranas* present a body of traditional material through myth and legend. There are eighteen *Puranas* in all, six each relating to Vishnu, Siva and Brahma which are in quality *sattvic* (pure), *tamasic* (gloomy) and *rajasic* (passionate), respectively. In addition to these *Maha-Puranas*, there are eighteen (or more) *Upa-Puranas*.

Ranke, Leopold von (1795–1896). Leading German historian of the nineteenth century who evolved a highly influential technique of philological and historical textual criticism. He made a mark on Western historiography with his research on particular limited periods of history while nursing a concern for the universal. In recognition of his work he was ennobled with the addition of 'von' to his name in 1865.

Roy, Manabendra Nath (1887–1954). This was the name—M.N. Roy in short—that Narendra Nath Bhattacharya adopted to evade British intelligence in the course of his revolutionary career. As a young radical in Bengal, he came under the influence of Jatindra Nath Mukherjee or Bagha Jatin. From 1915 onwards M.N. Roy became an activist in the international arena, developing an interest in Marxism and founding the Communist Party of Mexico. In July 1920, Roy was invited to the Second Comintern Congress in Moscow where he was received cordially by Lenin. In October of that year Roy formed the émigré Communist Party of India. He served as a member of the Comintern Presidium for eight years until he was expelled from it after falling out with Stalin. Back in India, Roy urged Indian communists to join ranks with the Congress Party in order to radicalize it. In the last phase of his life M.N. Roy was disillusioned with both communism and bourgeois democracy, and evolved an alternative philosophy which he called Radical Humanism.

Sankhya. One of the six orthodox systems of Indian philosophy ascribed to the sage Kapila. It takes its name from its numeral or discriminative tendencies. It is a synthetic system and is based on the principle of dualism. The two ultimate realities recognized by *Sankhya* are the *purusha*, the spirit, the intelligent principle whose essence is consciousness and *prakriti*, matter, the ultimate cause of the world and the eternal unconscious principle. *Purusha* and *prakriti* have generally been thought to represent the male and the female principles. *Sankhya* and *Yoga* form a pair like *Nyaya* and *Vaiseshika*, the third pair of the three great divisions of Hindu philosophy being *Mimamsa* (or *Purva-mimamsa*) and *Vedanta* (or *Uttara -mimamsa*).

Satya, Treta, Dwapar, Kali. Traditional Hindu chronology divides time into four *yugas* or epochs—*Krita* or *Satya, Treta, Dwapar* and *Kali*—the successive ages manifesting a progressive deterioration in values and morality. *Kali* is supposed to be the fallen millennium.

Shaftesbury, 7th Earl of, Anthony Ashley Cooper (1801–1885). Leader of the evangelical movement in the Church of England, Shaftesbury was also in the forefront of social and industrial reforms in nineteenth-century England. Although he was against the Reform Bill of 1832 for widening the franchise, Shaftesbury can be credited with a number of liberal moves such as supporting the repeal of the Corn Laws in 1846, ensuring passage of the Lunacy Act of 1845 which treated lunatics as 'persons of unsound mind' rather than social pariahs, working for factory reform legislation and shortening of the working day in textile mills (the Ten Hours Act was passed in 1847), and securing the passing of the Mines Act of 1842 excluding women, and girls and boys under ten years of age, from working in pits.

Shitala. *Ma Shitala* or *Shitala Devi* is the Hindu goddess of small pox representing both the disease and the cure.

Sismondi, Jean Charles Leonard Simonde de (1773–1842). Swiss economist and historian who was alive to the dangers of runaway industrialism. Remarkably farsighted, he foresaw the risks of limitless competition, overproduction and underconsumption. Though initially a loyal follower of Adam Smith, he later moved away from *laissez-faire* economics and argued for governmental regulation of economic competition. He also predicted a growing rift between the bourgeoisie and the working class, and advocated social reforms to improve the conditions of workers. He was naturally highly regarded by both Marx and Keynes. His monumental sixteen-volume history of the Italian republics in the Middle Ages was an inspiring force behind the movement for the unification of Italy.

Smriti. That which has been remembered and handed down by tradition. In its widest application, the term includes the *Vedangas*, the *Sutras*, the *Ramayana*, the *Mahabharata*, the *Puranas*, the *Nitisastras* and the *Dharmasastras*, especially the works of Manu, Yajnavalkya and the sixteen succeeding inspired law-givers. But its narrower application is only to the *Dharmasastras*. As Manu says, 'By *Sruti* is meant the *Veda*, and by *Smriti* the institutes of law.'

Solvay, Ernest (1838–1922). Belgian industrial chemist known for developing the ammonia-soda process for producing sodium carbonate, and philanthropist who founded institutes of scientific research in chemistry, physics and sociology. His over-riding passion for science was expressed when he organized a conference in Brussels in 1911 inviting most of the famous physicists and chemists of the time.

Sombart, Werner (1863–1941). German historical economist who was initially a Marxist but later became strongly anti-Marxist. The influence of Marx is evident in his work *Modern Capitalism* (1902). Here and in his later studies he proffered an evolutionary view of capitalism. The three stages of evolution, according to him, are the phase of the pre-Industrial Revolution merchant adventurer, the entrepreneurial phase and the cooperative phase.

Sorel, George-Eugene (1847–1922). French socialist and supporter, up to 1909, of revolutionary syndicalism, a movement leaning towards anarchism. Sorel developed a theory of the constructive role of myth and violence in the history of mankind (*Reflections on Violence*, 1908). His theory was later used perversely by Benito Mussolini.

Spencer, Herbert (1820–1903). English sociologist and philosopher who applied the biological conception of evolution to sociological theory, and who generally advocated the examination of social phenomena in a scientific way. His great work was *The Synthetic Philosophy* (1855–96) with its many volumes devoted to the principles of psychology, biology, ethics and sociology.

Spengler, Oswald (1880–1936). German philosopher who is famous for his contribution to social theory in his two-volume study, *The Decline of the West* (1918–22). He believed that most civilizations must pass through a life cycle, and that the West had already passed from the creative stage of culture to a stage of reflection and material comfort, with the future inevitably poised to be a stage of decline. Civilizations, according to him, blossom and decay like natural organisms.

Sruti. That which has been heard, i.e. the revealed word that has been directly communicated to certain *rishis*. The term is properly only applied to the *Mantra* and *Brahmana* portion of the *Vedas*, although it has been extended to include the *Upanishads* and other Vedic works.

Taine, Hippolyte Adolphe (1829–1893). French thinker, critic and historian, and an exponent of nineteenth-century French positivism. He attempted to apply the scientific method to the study of the humanities. Taine's formidable reputation as an intellectual and man of letters rests on his works on La Fontaine, Livy, the French philosophers of the nineteenth century and his *History of English Literature* in four volumes (1856–59).

Tawney, Richard Henry (1880–1962). Economic historian, social critic and educationist. Born in Calcutta, the son of a Sanskrit scholar, Tawney was educated at Rugby School and Balliol College, Oxford. From 1920 to 1949 he taught at the London School of Economics. Tawney helped to shape the important report, 'The Education of the Adolescent', which became the basis for the Education Act of 1944. He was also active in the matter of the role of the Church of England in social teaching. His vision of socialism was informed by Christian morality. As a historian he is known for his classic works, *The Acquisitive Society* (1921), *Religion and the Rise of Capitalism* (1926) and *Equality* (1931). His scholarly work on the economic history of England is so widely acknowledged that the years 1540–1640 are known as 'Tawney's century'.

Thoreau, Henry David (1817–1862). American essayist, poet and practical philosopher who imbibed the doctrines of Transcendentalism from his friend Ralph Waldo Emerson. His master work, *Walden* (1854), is a record of his ardent love of nature and acute observation of natural phenomena. He was a vigorous champion of civil liberties, and his essay on 'Civil Disobedience' (1849) has been a source of inspiration for Mahatma Gandhi and many civil rights leaders.

Tortoise incarnation. Vishnu is said to visit the earth in ten incarnations. These are *Narasimha* or the Lion Man, *Vamana* or Dwarf, Rama, *Kurma* or Tortoise, *Matsya* or Fish, *Varaha* or Boar, Parasurama, Balarama and Buddha. In the *Kali Yuga* he appears as *Kalki* incarnation.

Varnasrama. The *Manu Dharmasastra* divided society into four socially separate occupational categories which formed the basis of the caste system among Hindus. The *chaturvarna* or four castes are the *Brahmana* (the sacerdotal and learned class, members of which may be, but are not necessarily, priests), the *Kshatriya* (the regal and warrior class), the *Vaisya* (trading and agricultural caste) and the *Sudra* (the lowest caste whose duty is to serve the other three).

Webb, Sidney (1859–1947). Sidney Webb and his wife Beatrice Webb (1858–1943) were co-founders of the London School of Economics and Political Science. The two were also pioneers in social and economic reforms, and left a mark on English social thought and institutions. An early member of the Fabian Society, which he joined on Bernard Shaw's insistence, Sidney Webb later came to be associated with the Labour Party. Sidney and Beatrice have left behind such monuments of historical research as The *History of Trade Unionism* (1894), *Industrial Democracy* (1897), and a history of English local government from the seventeenth to the twentieth century published over a period of twenty-five years.

Weber, Max (1864–1920). Regarded as one of the founders of modern sociology as a distinct science, Weber held that sociology gives an interpretative account of social action using an 'ideal-type' methodology. Presenting rationalization as the master trend of Western capitalist society, he saw Protestantism not as a direct cause of capitalism but as preparing a culture emphasizing industry, frugality, punctuality and honest dealings in the pursuit of wealth. He also contributed to the sociology of comparative religions, urban sociology, economic history, sociology of music and of law, and the analysis of ancient civilization. Among his voluminous publications are *Economy and Society* (1922), *The Protestant Ethic and the Spirit of Capitalism* (1905), *General Economic History* (1923), *Religion of China* (1916), *Religion of India* (1916–17) and *Ancient Judaism* (1917–19).

Whitehead, Alfred North (1861–1947). English mathematician, philosopher and educationist. Whitehead was a teacher in Trinity College, Cambridge, when he was struck by the brilliance of Bertrand Russell whom he examined for an entrance scholarship at Cambridge. The two became close friends and collaborated in writing *Principia Mathematica* (1910–13). Moving to London, Whitehead wrote *An Introduction to Mathematics* (1911), which is read even today. In 1914 he became professor of applied mathematics at the Imperial College of Science and Technology, and in 1924, professor of philosophy at Harvard. His *Process and Reality* (1929) is considered to be one of the greatest books of Western metaphysics.